Foundation Biology

For Class X

Part-1 of 2

NOTION PRESS

NOTION PRESS

India. Singapore. Malaysia.

ISBN xxx-x-xxxxx-xx-x

Dedicated to our Beloved Prime Minister Shree Narendra Modi ji, whose life gives the Inspiration to every Individual

*If a Man **Decides** to achieve something in his life nothing is Impossible*

कर्मण्येवाधिकारस्ते मा फलेषु कदाचन।

मा कर्मफलहेतुर्भूर्मा ते सङ्गोऽस्त्वकर्मणि॥ २-४७

Karmanye vadhikaraste Ma Phaleshu Kadachana,

Ma Karmaphalaheturbhurma Te Sangostvakarmani

You have the right to work only but never to its fruits.

Let not the fruits of action be your motive, nor let your attachment be to inaction.

TOPIC NAME	PAGE NO.

1. LIFE PROCESS

TOPIC NAME	PAGE NO.

2. CONTROL AND COORDINATION

PRECISE

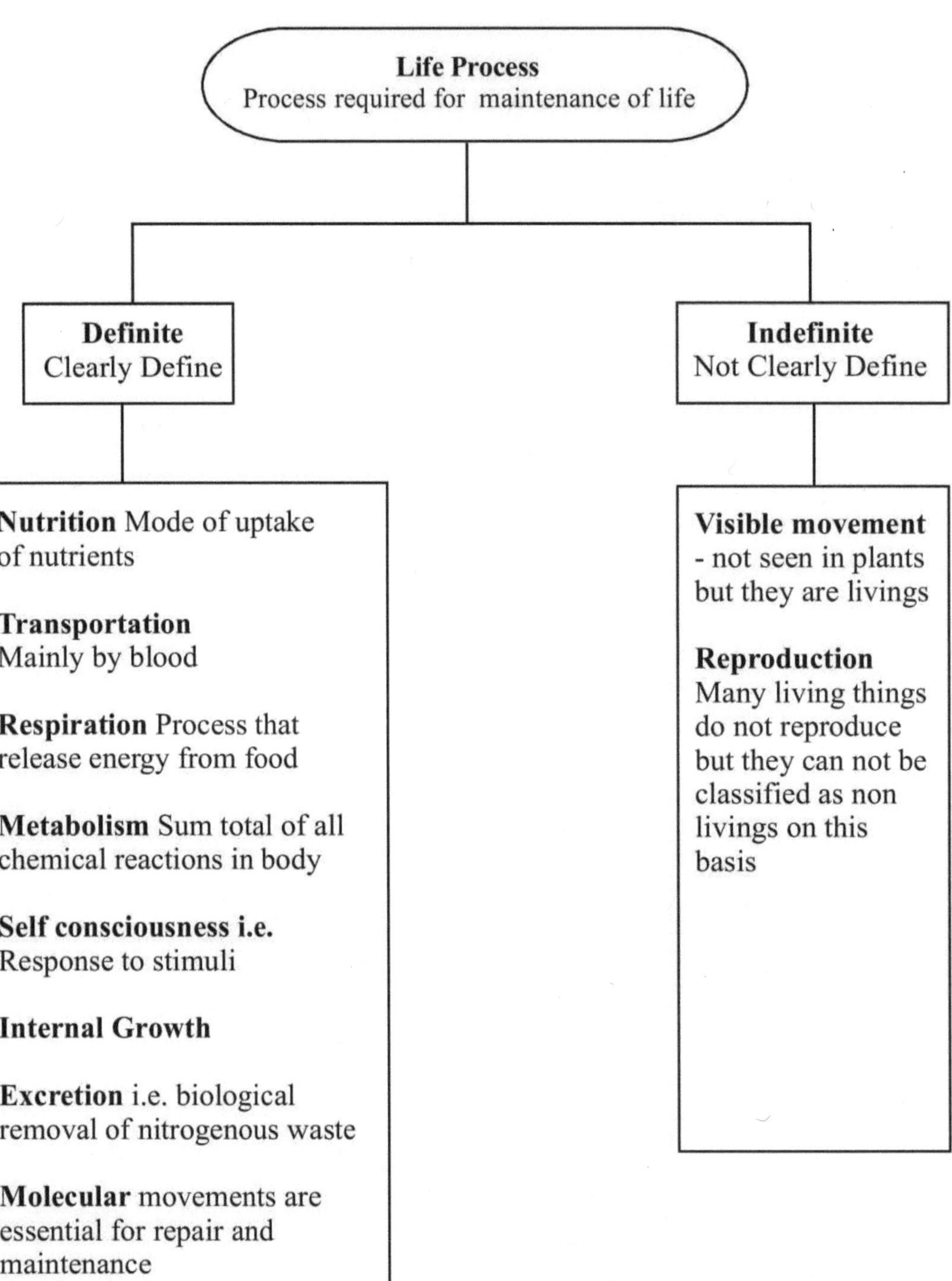
Life Process
Process required for maintenance of life
Definite
Clearly Define
Indefinite
Not Clearly Define
Nutrition Mode of uptake of nutrients
Transportation Mainly by blood
Respiration Process that release energy from food
Metabolism Sum total of all chemical reactions in body
Self consciousness i.e. Response to stimuli
Internal Growth
Excretion i.e. biological removal of nitrogenous waste
Molecular movements are essential for repair and maintenance
Visible movement - not seen in plants but they are livings
Reproduction Many living things do not reproduce but they can not be classified as non livings on this basis

1 LIFE PROCESS

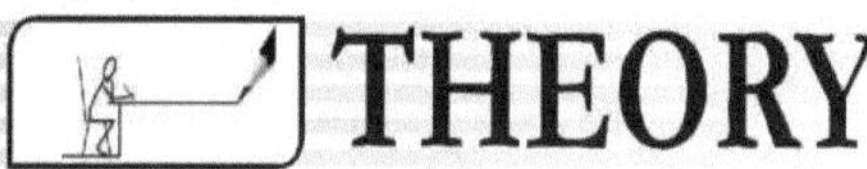

THEORY

INTRODUCTION

- **Life :** Life is a self regulated complex system of molecules where chemical reactions are going on all the time that lead to its maintinance, growth, responsiveness and reproduction.
- **Living organism :** Living beings are organised self regulated discrete entities which exhibit the various characteristic of life like movements, growth, responsiveness and reproduction.
- **Life processes :** All the living organisms including humans perform a number of activities such as nutrition, respiration, excretion, growth & reproduction. These activities are characteristics of living organism & help in maintenance of life. These maintenance functions of living organisms are known as **life processes**.

Some Characteristic of living organisms

(i) **Cellular organization :** All organisms are made up of cells.

(ii) **Sensitivity :** Giving response to stimuli (Stimulus = change in environment) (Response = visible effect because of stimulus) Consciousness is one of the most important definite life feature. ***eg.*** Plants grows towards light, pupil dilate in dark etc.

(iii) **Respiration & Energy utilization:** Respiration is the process in which nutrients are converted into useful energy in a cell. Energy produced during respiration is used to perform many kinds of works with in the body.

(iv) **Internal growth:**It is characteristic feature of livings.

(v) **Homeostasis:** All organism maintain relatively constant internal conditions in different environments, known as homeostasis.

(vi) **Regulation:** All organism have neural or chemical regulatory mechanism that co-ordinate internal processes.

(vii) **Reproduction:** It is a process of producing young ones of their own kinds. Heredity character are passed from parent to the offsprings during reproduction.

(viii) **Metabolism:** The sum total of all the chemical & physical changes that are constantly taking place in living organisms & are necessary for life.

Types of metabolic pathways

(a) **Anabolic pathways :** Biosynthetic pathways, in which complex substances are synthesized from simpler ones. Ex : Photosynthesis (Endothermic reaction – energy is used)

(b) **Catabolic pathways** : Break down of complex organic substances into simpler ones. Ex : Respiration. (Exothermic – energy released)

(ix) **Excretion :** A number of waste products are formed as by-products of metabolism. They are usually toxic and removed from the body.

(x) **Irritability :** Every living organism is aware of its surroundings. It responds to changes in the environment. **The branch of biology that deals with the study of life process, activities and body functions is called physiology.**

NUTRITION

"Nutrition" is a process of intake as well as utilization of nutrients by an organism. It is the process of breakdown of nutrients into smaller molecules and their absorption. Food provides us nutrition and energy. It contains different types of nutrients in varying amounts according to the need of our body.

Nutrients :

These are the substances required by our body for its growth, repair, work and maintenance of the body. Different types of nutrients are carbohydrates, fats, proteins, vitamins, mineral etc. Our daily energy need may vary according to our occupation, age, sex and under some specific conditions.

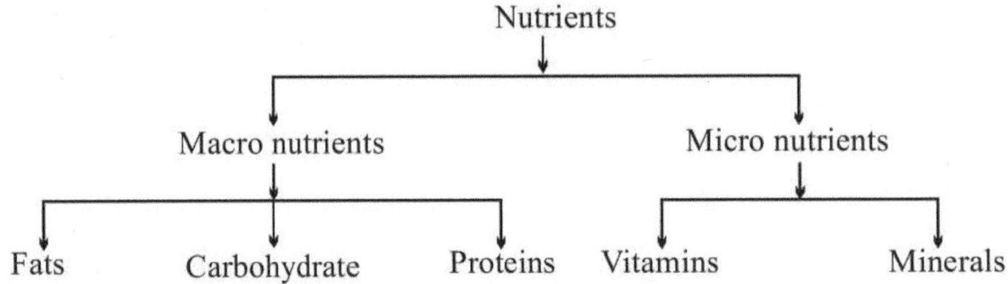

MODES OF NUTRITION :

- There are several modes of nutrition on the basis of which organisms are classified as follows :

1. Autotrophic : (Auto = self, trophic = food)

- It is a mode of nutrition in which organisms prepare their own food.
- Inorganic molecules like CO_2 and H_2O are converted into organic molecules like carbohydrates in the presence of sunlight and chlorophyll. e.g. Green plants. Autotrophs are further categorized. as:
  (i) Photoautotroph : Those which utilize sunlight for preparing their food
  (ii) Chemoautotroph : Those which utilize chemical energy for preparing their food.

2. Heterotrophic : (Hetero = different ; trophic = food)

- It is a mode of nutrition in which organisms derive their food from some other animals or plants.
- They cannot prepare their own food e.g. human being. Heterotrophs are further categorized depending on the nature of food they consume :
  (i) **Herbivores :** Animals which eat only plants, e.g. Cow, goat etc.
  (ii) **Carnivores :** They feed on flesh of other animals, e.g. Lion, vulture etc.
  (iii) **Omnivores :** They feed on plants and animals both e.g. Dog, human etc.
  (iv) **Detritivores :** Feed on detritus or dead organic remains, e.g. Earthworm etc.
  (v) **Sanguivorous :** Feed on blood e.g. Leech, female mosquito etc.
  (vi) **Frugivorous :** Feed on fruits, e.g. Parrot etc.
  (vii) **Insectivores :** Feed on insects, e.g. Bats etc.

On the Basis of Mode of Feeding Organisms are Categorised As :

(i) **Holozoic :** They ingest mostly solid but sometimes liquid food. e.g., Amoeba, human etc.

(ii) **Saprotrophic :** They absorb organic matter from dead and decaying organisms with the help of their enzymes. e.g., Bacteria, fungi etc.

(iii) **Parasitic :** They derive their nutrition from other living plants or animals e.g. Plasmodium, round worms, etc.

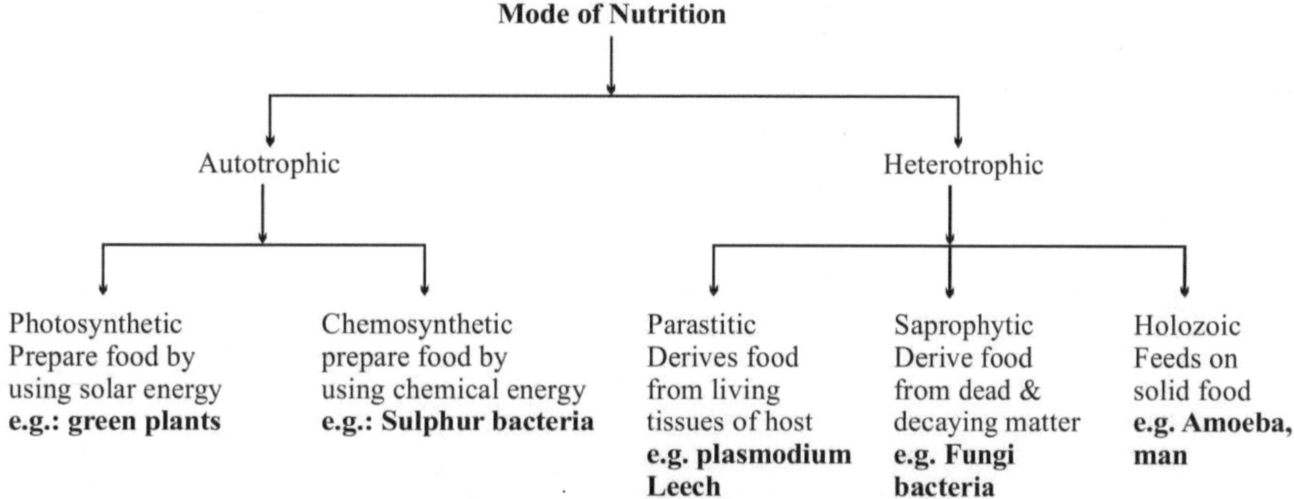

- **Nutrition can be divided into two categories on the basis of occurance.**
  1. Nutrition in plants 2. Nutrition in animals.

NUTRITION IN PLANTS

- Plant perform photosynthesis [Photo (light) and synthesis (Build up)]. **Photosynthesis is a process that converts carbon dioxide into organic compounds, especially sugars, using sunlight in presence of chlorophyll. Photosynthesis occurs in plants, algae, and many species of bacteria.** It is represented by:

$$6CO_2 + 12H_2O + \text{Sunlight} \xrightarrow{\text{Chlorophyll}} C_6H_{12}O_6 + 6O_2\uparrow + 6H_2O$$

- It takes place in every green part of plant mainly in the green leaves. Plants stores food in the form of **Starch**.
  [Different from animals which stores food in the form of **Glycogen**]

Factors involved in Photosynthesis

1. Sunlight :

- For plants, sun is the basic source of radiant energy.
- Plants utilize the light in the visible region of solar spectra (electromagnetic spectrum) which comes under the range of 380 nm - 780 nm.
- Visible region consists of white light which is a mixture of 7 lights of different wavelengths.

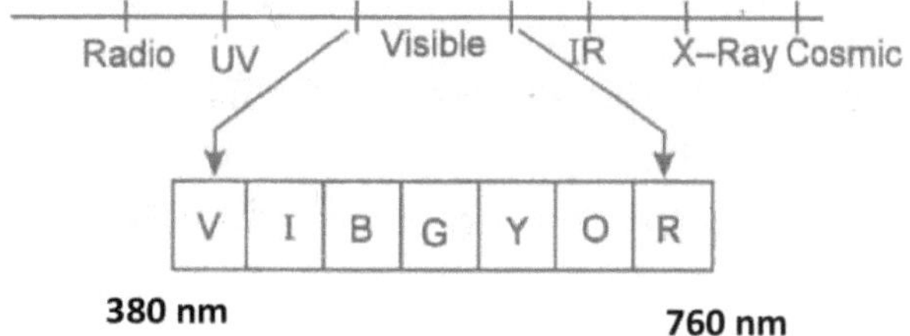

Note : Plants utilize carbon dioxide during photosynthesis, the intensity of light at which amount of CO_2 used during photosynthesis becomes equal to the amount of CO_2 released during respiration by plants in called as **Compensation point**.

Compensation point occurs at low light intensity that is during morning and during evening hours.

Sunlight ——————→ **VIBGYOR**
Red/Orange → Maximum Photosynthesis
Blue/violet → Highest rate of absorption
Green → No Photosynthesis

Starch test : Requirement for photosynthesis can be tested by reaction between starch and iodine refer as starch test.

Starch + I_2 → Blue Black Colour

Steps of starch test

1. Heat some water to boiling point in a beaker .
2. Use forceps to dip a leaf in the hot water for about 30 seconds. This kills the cytoplasm, denatures the enzymes and makes the leaf more permeable to iodine solution.
3. Push the leaf to the bottom of a test tube and cover it with alcohol. Place the tube in the hot water (water bath). The alcohol will boil and dissolve out most of the chlorophyll.
4. Remove the leaf and dip it once into the hot water to soften it.
5. Spread the decolorized leaf flat on a white tile and drop iodine solution onto it. The parts containing starch will turn blue; parts without starch will stain brown or yellow with iodine.

- Covered part will show Brown/Yellow while uncovered part will show blue black colour
- This proves light is essential for photosynthesis.

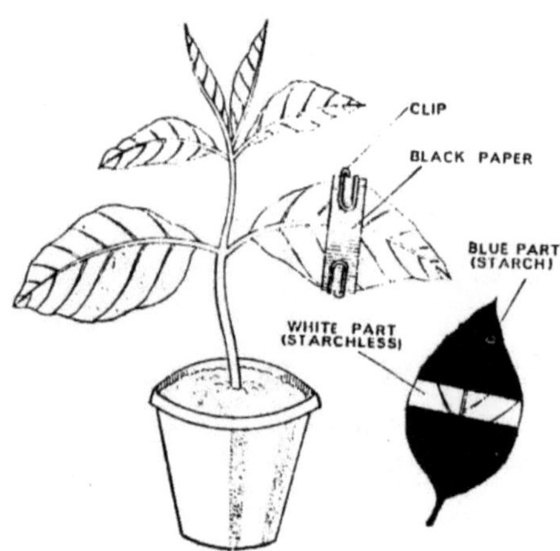

2. Carbon-di-oxide :

- Terrestrial plants obtain carbon dioxide from the atmosphere through the small openings present on leaves called as **stomata**.
- They help in exchange of gases and water.
- Stomata opening is guarded by the presence of guard cells (kidney shaped).
- Aquatic plants obtain CO_2 dissolved in water through their general body surface so they perform more photosynthesis than terrestrial plants.

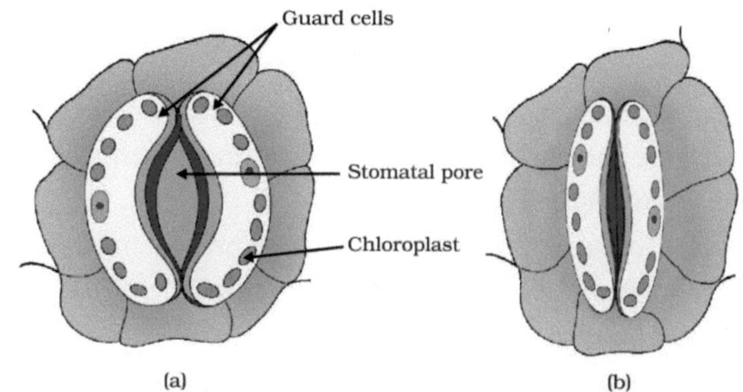

Test : To prove CO_2 is essential for photosynthesis.

- Take a test tube and put some KOH(KOH absorbs CO_2) inside the tube. Cover its mouth with perforated cork.
- Insert half part of leaf inside tube (Inner portion is devoid of CO_2 while outer part receive CO_2).
- Make assembly air tight with help of vaseline.
- Perform starch test.
- Inner part will remain Brown/Yellow while outer part will show blue black colour.

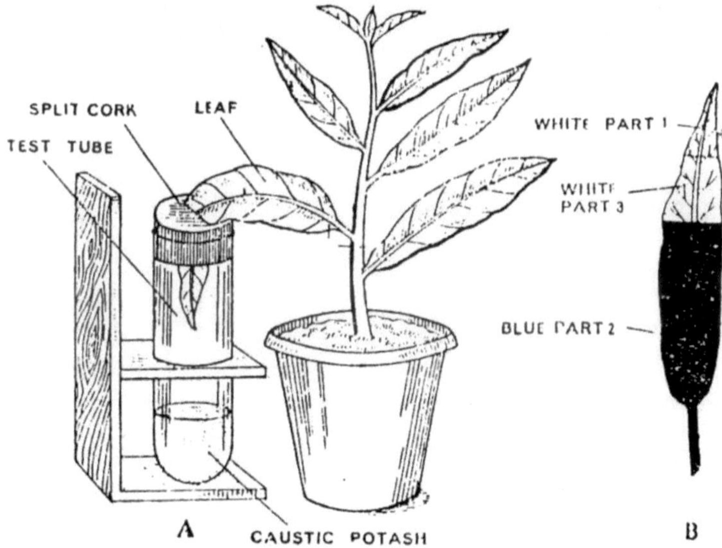

- It can also be performed by Bell-Jars experiment.

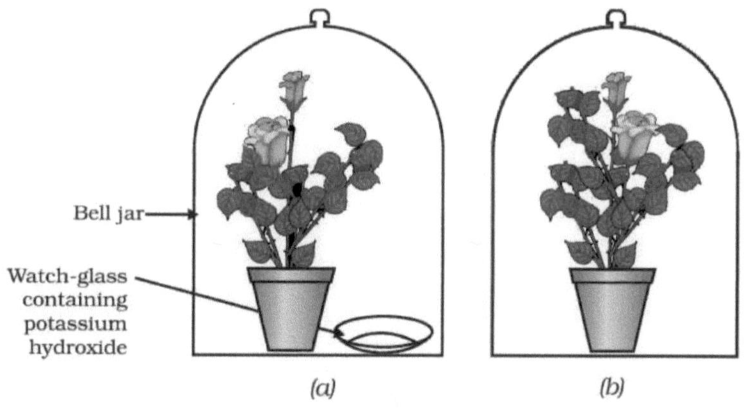

3. Chlorophyll :

These are the green pigments present in chloroplast. They are found in green leaves in a maximum amount as well as in other green aerial parts of plant. There are six different types of chlorophyll, they are chlorophyll a,b,c,d,e and bacteriochlorophyll, amongst them chlorophyll a and chlorophyll b are the most commonly occurring chlorophylls.

Besides chlorophyll certain other pigments are also present in plants like.

(i) Carotenes : Orange in colour e.g. Carrot.

(ii) Xanthophylls : Orange yellow in colour e.g. Maize.

(iii) Phycobilins : Different colour like red, violet e.g. Blue-green algae, brown algae etc.

Table – Kinds of Photosynthetic pigments in various groups of plants

Photosynthetic Pigment	Colour	Distribution
Chlorophyll		
(i) Chlorophyll a	yellow green	All green plants except bacteria
(ii) Chlorophyll b	blue green	All higher plants and green algae
(iii) Chlorophyll c	green	Diatoms
(iv) Chlorophyll d	green / red	Red algae
(v) Bacteriochlorophylls	pale blue	Bacteria
Carotenoids		
Carotenes and Xanthophylls	orange	Algae and higher plants
Phycobilins		
Phycoerythrin	red	Red algae
Phycocyanin	red	Red algae and blue green algae

- Take a variegated (multi colour) leaf like Crotons. Mark green and non green areas.
- Perform starch test.
- Non green part will show Brown/Yellow while green part will show blue black colour.
- This proves chlorophyll is essential for photosynthesis.

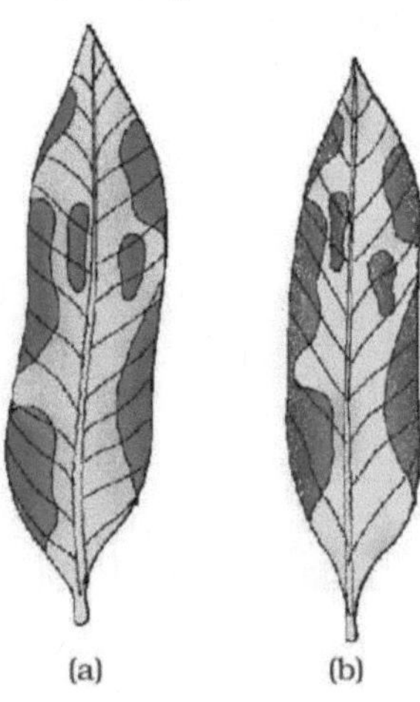

4. Water

Plants absorb water by root hairs from the soil by the process of osmosis which get transported upward through xylem to the leaves. It act as an important raw material and helps in production of reducing power that is $NADH_2$ and $FADH_2$.

- Besides that various enzymes are also involved in photosynthesis.

SITE OF PHOTOSYNETHESIS :

- The actual site of photosynthesis is chloroplast (cell organelle)
- **Leaf → Mesophyll tissue → Palisade / Spongy parenchyma →Chloroplast → Chlorophyll**
- **Green** colour of plants appears because out of the **seven colour** of the **white visible light,** chlorophyll absorb all excepts **green colour.** Green is totally **reflected back.** Hence, leaves look **green** in colour.

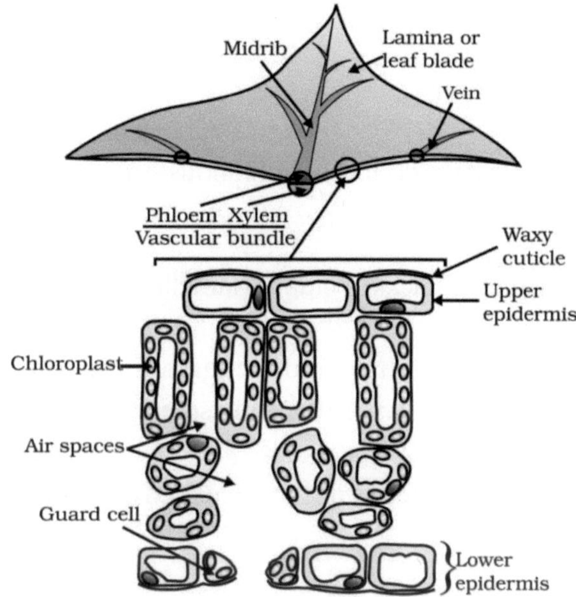

Site of photosynthesis is different in prokaryotes and eukaryotes.

- **In prokaryotes :** Photosynthesis occurs in lamellar chromatophores.
- **In eukaryotes :** Photosynthesis occurs in chloroplast.
- **Exception :** Fungi (It lacks chlorophyll so no photosynthesis occurs here).
- In higher plants chloroplast in the main site of photosynthesis.
- Chloroplast is also called as green plastid.
- Plastid was first observed by **Haeckel**.
- Plastids are of 3 different types on the basis of pigments present in them.

(i) **Leucoplast :** White in colour, found in underground parts, lacks coloured pigment. Helps in storage of protein (Aleuroplst), oil (Elaioplast), starch (Amyloplast)

(ii) **Chromoplast :** Colour other than green found in aerial parts on the plants.

(iii) **Chloroplast :**

- Contain green pigment, called as **chlorophyll**.
- Chloroplast was discovered by **Schimper**.
- Number of chloroplasts is variable in different species of plants.
- In lower plants like algae they are 1 or 2 number.
- In higher plants their number varies from 40 - 100 per palisade cell or more.

- Chloroplast also have variable shapes, for example cup shaped, ribbon shaped etc. in algae while it is discoidal in higher plants.

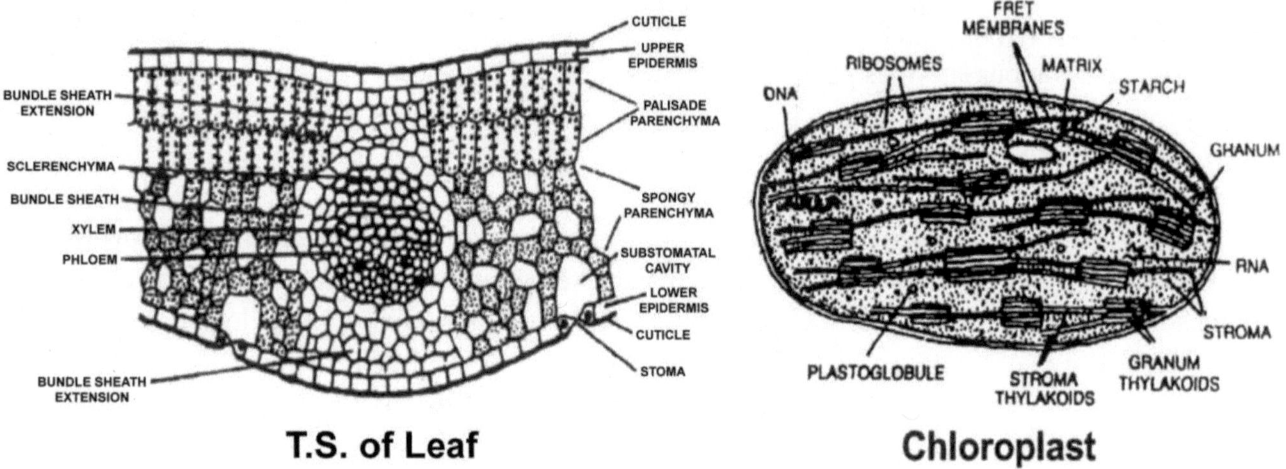

T.S. of Leaf

Chloroplast

- A typical structure of chloroplast is a double membranous structure having two parts.

(a) Grana :

- It is a lamellar system consisting of stacks of granum lamella each bounded by a membranous box called as **thylakoid**.
- They are 40 - 60 per cell. Number of thylakoids per grana is 50 or more Chlorophyll molecules are found inside the thylakoid membrane where they trap solar energy in the form of small energy packets called **'photon'** or **'quanta'**.
- Grana are interconnected to each other by a channel called as **stroma lamellae** or **Fret's channel**.

(b) Stroma :

- It is a non pigmented proteinaceous matrix in which grana remain embedded. It contain enzymes for dark reaction.

Structure of Chlorophyll molecule :

- A chlorophyll molecule has two parts.
  (i) A tetrapyrrole ring or a porphyrin ring and
  (ii) A long hydrocarbon tail called phytol.
  – The porphyrin ring has four smaller pyrrole rings.
  – In each small ring there is a nitrogen atom.
  – All four rings bind with a metal atom magnesium (Mg^{++}) present at the centre.
  – A porphyrin ring called the head has a flat structure with alternate single and double bonds.
  – The head joins with the tail by an ester linkage
  – A porphyrin ring has number of side-chains.
  – The side-chains differ in different chlorophylls like chlorophyll a has a methyl group ($-CH_3$) and Chlorophyll b has an aldehyde group (–CHO) Refer Fig. These side chains modify the absorption spectrum also.
- Chlorophyll *a* is more abundant in green plants than chlorophyll *b*.

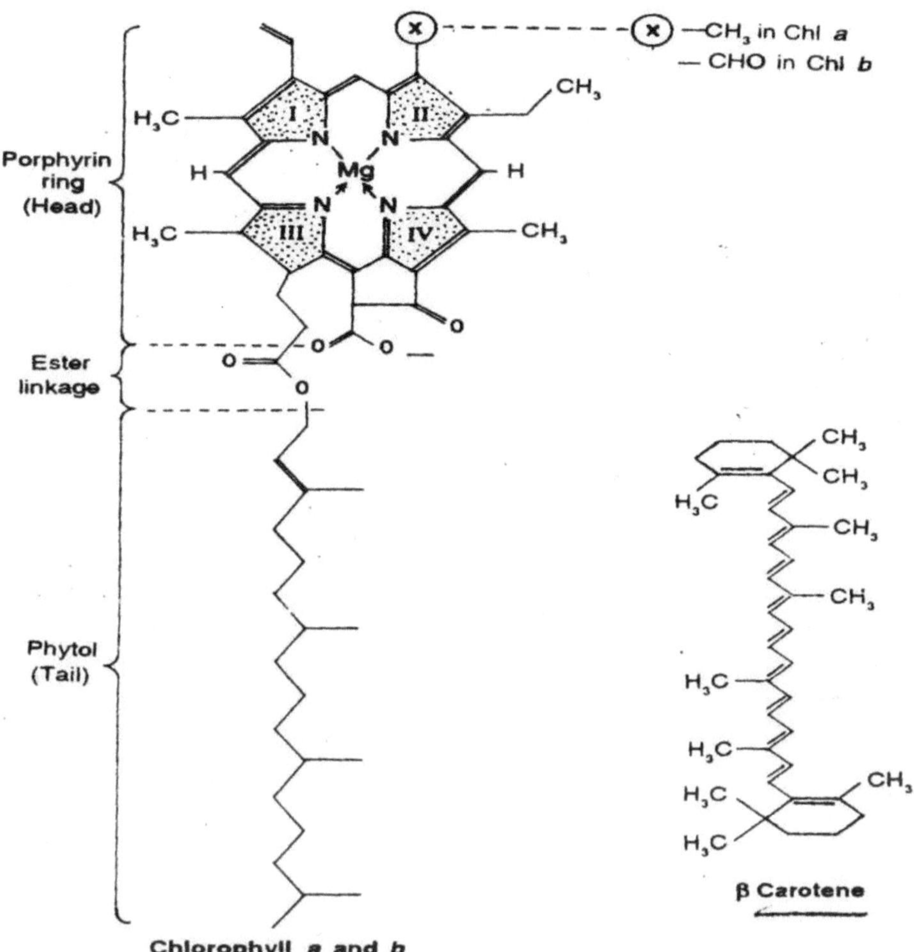

Structure of Chlorophyll *a*, Chlorophyll *b* and β Carotene

MECHANISM OF PHOTOSYNTHESIS :

(I) LIGHT REACTION :

- It is also called as photochemical process.
- It was discovered by **'Robert Hill'** therefore it is also called as **Hill's reaction**.
- **Site :** Grana of chloroplast.
- **Raw materials :** Light and water.
- **Regulation :** This process is regulated by chlorophyll molecules.

It involves three basic steps :

(A) Photo excitation of chlorophyll molecule :

During this process chlorophyll molecule receives sunlight in the form of small energy bundles called as photons and become excited to higher energy level.

(B) Photolysis :

- It is also called as photoxidation of water, this takes place in presence of Mn^{+2} and Cl^{-} ions.

- O_2 is liberated as by product and H^+ ions are used for reduction of NADP

$$2NADP + 4H \rightarrow 2NADPH_2$$

(C) Photophosphorylation :

- During this process ATP are produced. It takes place in quantasomes.
- Mg^{+2} ions and inorganic phosphate is required to convert ADP into ATP, $ADP + iP \rightarrow ATP$.

(II) DARK REACTION :

- It is also called as thermo chemical reaction.
- It was discovered by Melvin calvin and Benson therefore it is also called as
- Calvin cycle Site = Stroma of chloroplast.
- **Raw materials :** They require CO_2, $NADPH_2$, ATP and Enzymes.
- **Regulated by :** Light reaction and enzymes.

It involves three basic steps :

(A) Carboxylation :

In this step CO_2 is captured by CO_2 acceptors like RUBP (C_3 Plants) PEP (C_4 Plants) with the help of carboxylase enzyme i.e. RUBISCO & PEPCO respectively.

(B) Synthesis :

This phase capture CO_2 is assimilated into glucose in the presence of phosphatase and isomerease enzymes and RUBP is regenerated back.

(C) Regeneration of RUBP

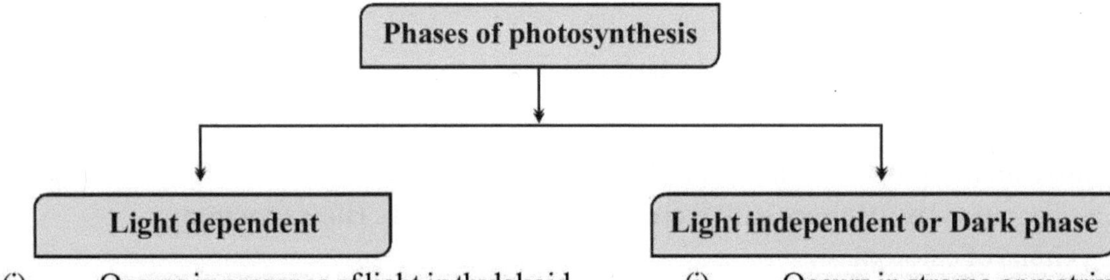

Light dependent

(i) Occurs in presence of light in thylakoid.

(ii) Excitation of chlorophyll by light.

(iii) Electron moves in cytochrome system.

(iv) Light energy in converted into chemical energy (ATP).

(v) Photolysis of water (O_2 is released).

(vi) ATP, $NADPH_2$, O_2 are the main end products of light reaction.

Light independent or Dark phase

(i) Occurs in stroma or matrix. Use products of light reaction.

(ii) RUBP* acts as acceptor of CO_2

(iii) Using ATP and *$NADPH_2$, CO_2 is reduced to carbohydrate.

Diffirence between light reaction & Dark reaction

	Light Reaction	Dark Reaction
1. Light	It is required for the reaction	It is light independent.
2. Conversion	The reaction converts light energy into chemical energy.	The reaction uses chemical energy in building organic.
3. Chlorophyll	It is essential for the reaction.	Chlorophyll is not required directly.
4. Occurance	It occurs in thylakoids of chloroplasts.	It occurs in stroma part of chloroplasts.
5. Products	Its products are ATP and $NADPH_2$	Its main product is starch.
6. Oxygen	Oxygen is liberated as a by product.	Its does not produce oxygen.
7. Electron transport	Light reaction involves movement of electrons along a transport chain.	There is no involvement of an electron transport chain.

OVERALL REACTION OF DARK PHASE :

$12RUBP + 6CO_2 + 12NADPH + 18ATP + 12H^+ \rightarrow 12RUBP + C_6H_{12}O_6 + 18ADP + 18ip + 12NADP$

* **RUBP** = Ribulose Bi Phosphate
* **NADP = Nicotinamide Adenine Dinucleotide Phosphate**
* **ip = Inorganic phosphate**

- Desert plants are exception. They open stomata in night to absorb CO_2 and form intermediate compound i.e. **malate**. Which is stored in vacuole and during day it is converted into sugar.

FACTORS AFFECTING PHOTOSYNTHESIS :

(a) Light :

- Normally plants utilize sunlight but marine algae can perform photosynthesis even in the moon light.
- Plants can also perform photosynthesis in the artificial lights.
- Highest rate of photosynthesis : Red light
- Minimum photosynthesis : Green light
- Very high light intensity can cause reduction in the rate of photosynthesis by causing
  (i) Decrease in transpiration rate (ii) Denaturation of chlorophyll molecule

(b) Temperature :

- Optimum range = 25°C to 30°C
- It ranges from 10°C - 40°C
- In some forms like algae of hot spring 60°C - 70°C is normal

(c) Carbon dioxide :

- It is the raw material for the formation of glucose. Land plants obtain CO_2 from the atmosphere through the stomata. The aquatic plants get their CO_2 as bicarbonates through their general surface.
- CO_2 used by the green plants during photosynthesis is released due to respiration in green plants and other organisms.
- Hence, we say that photosynthesis and respiration are antagonistic to each other.
- It has been proved experimentally that an increases in CO_2 concentration up to 0.5 percent may cause increase in photosynthesis but only for a limited time period provided other conditions remain constant.

(d) Oxygen :

- O_2 acts as competitive inhibitor of CO_2. Over concentration of O_2 stops photosynthesis.

(e) Chlorophyll :

- Chlorophyll content is directly proportional to rate of photosynthesis. No photosynthesis occurs in etiolated cells, In variegated leaves it occurs only at places where chlorophyll is present.

SIGNIFICANCE OF PHOTOSYNTHESIS :

- Photosynthesis is a boon to the nature and to the human beings. It has following significance :
  (i) Production of food material
  (ii) Atmospheric control and purification of air.

NUTRITION IN ANIMALS :

- Animal are heterotrophs (consumers). They depend upon plants or animals for food and can not synthesize their own food.

Holozoic nutrition :

- Holozoic nutrition is typical of most animals - all vertebrates and most invertebrates.
- The organisms take the whole food (animal or plant or their parts) into their body and then digest it to smaller particles.
- They have a specialised digestive tract which has various parts modified for ingestion, digestion, absorption and egestion.

Process of Nutrition in Animals : -

Ingestion → Digestion → Absorption → Assimilation → Egestion

1. Nutrition in Amoeba :

- Amoeba is holozoic (takes solid food). It is omnivorous i.e. it ingests all kinds of aquatic micro-organisms like bacteria, diatoms, algae, other protozoans, etc.

Steps of Nutrition in amoeba

(i) **Ingestion:** Food is taken in with help of pseudopodia
(ii) **Digestion:** Intracellular with help of enzymes present in lysosomes.
(iii) Absorption and Assimilation
(iv) **Egestion:** Undigested food thrown out

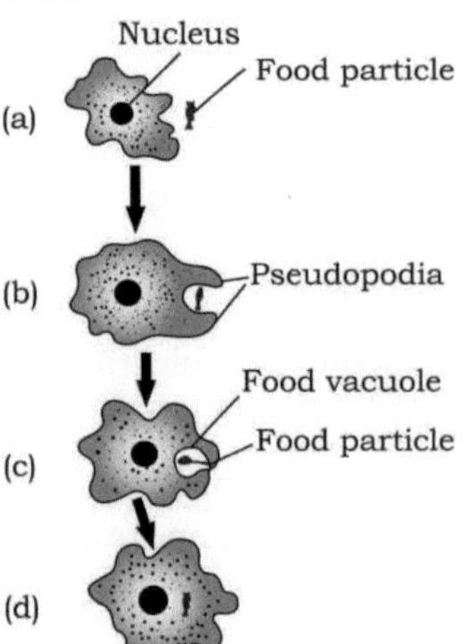

2. Nutrition in Human Being

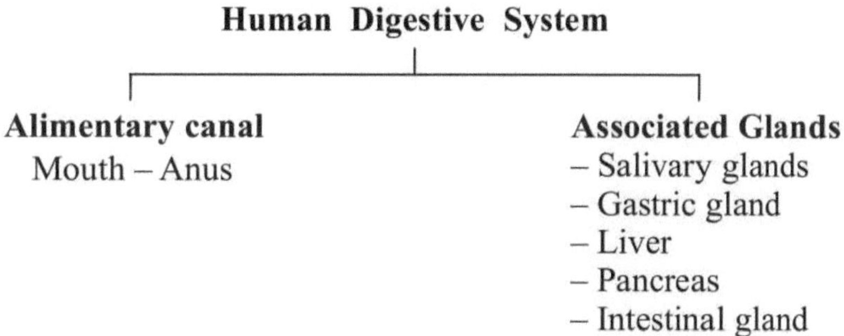

Mouth → Pharynx → Oesophagus → Stomach → Duodenum → Jejunum → Ileum → Ceacum → Colon → Rectum → Anus

DIGESTIVE SYSTEM OF MAN

- All the organs that are responsible for the intake of food, its digestion, assimilation and removal of the undigested waste in an organism constitute the digestive system. It is made up of :
  1. Alimentary canal
  2. Associated digestive glands

1. ALIMENTARY CANAL

Buccal Cavity -

- It is an organ of ingestion, mastication and swallowing of food.
- It consists of teeth, tongue, palate and its muscles. It opens outside through the mouth aperture.
- It lies below the nasal cavity and is separated from it by the palate.
- The hard palate forms the roof of the mouth and continues posteriorly into soft palate.
- The extension of soft palate in the form of uvula can be seen in an open mouth.
- Internally the buccal cavity is lined with mucous membrane containing mucus glands.
- There are 3 pairs of salivary glands which pour their secretions in the form of saliva in the mouth i.e.
  1. Parotid gland
  2. Submandibular
  3. Sub lingual

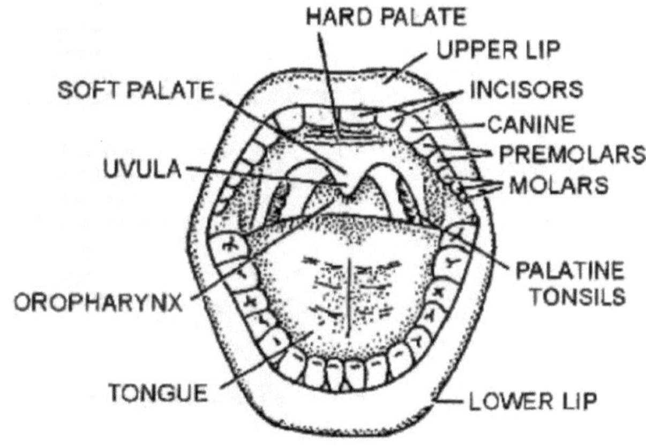

Fig. Buccal Cavity of Man

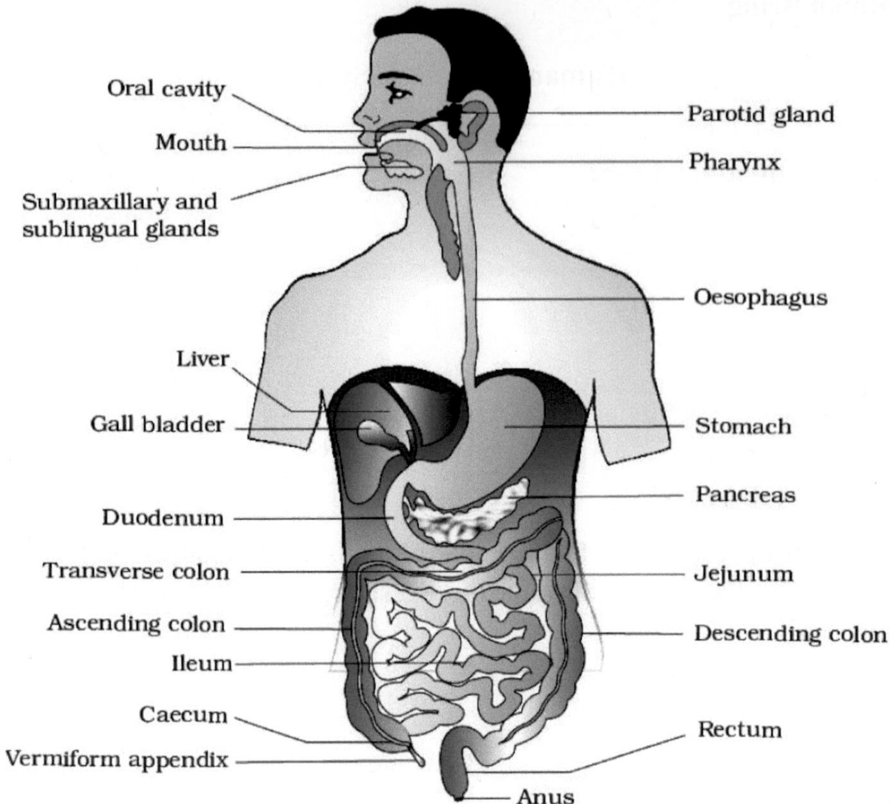

Fig. Human Digestive System

Teeth -

Jaws present in buccal cavity are provided with four different types of teeth (**Heterodont**) :

Incisors	:	For cutting
Canines	:	For tearing
Premolars	:	For grinding
Molars	:	For grinding

- Dental formula of humans : In human beings two set of teeth appear during their life time (**Diphyodont**)-

(A) Milk teeth : These are temporary , arise at 6 – 11 month age, 20 in number

$$\frac{\text{Half upper jaw}}{\text{Half lower jaw}} - = i\frac{2}{2},\ c\frac{1}{1},\ pm\frac{0}{0},\ m\frac{2}{2}$$

(B) Permanent teeth : In adults

$$\frac{\text{Half upper jaw}}{\text{Half lower jaw}} = i\frac{2}{2},\ c\frac{1}{1},\ pm\frac{2}{2},\ m\frac{3}{3}$$

Tongue-

- At the floor of the oral cavity is present a musculo-sensory organ, the tongue.
- It has voluntary muscles and is richly supplied with blood vessels and sensory neurons.
- On its surface are present tiny protuberances called **papillae**. These papillae have **taste buds** for identifying the chemical nature of food.
- Tongue is not only an organ of taste but also helps in swallowing the food and is essential for speech.

Pharynx-

- It is a wide opening at the back of mouth.
- Posteriorly it leads into two tubes - gullet (food pipe) and glottis (wind pipe).

- In front of glottis is a muscular flap epiglottis which closes the glottis when the food is swallowed.
- Pharynx has 2 openings of internal nares above and two opening of Eustachian tubes on the sides

Oesophagus-

- It is a long narrow muscular tube which connects mouth to stomach.
- Food passes through oesophagus by peristaltic movements of the muscular wall.

Stomach-

- It is a large muscular elastic bag situated below the diaphragm.
- Its walls are supplied with glandular epithelium secreting gastric juices and mucus.
- It is J shaped and is present on the left hand side of the abdomen. It has three parts- **cardiac**, **fundus**, and **pylorus**. Cardiac end is towards the oesophagus and food passes into the duodenum through the pylorus.

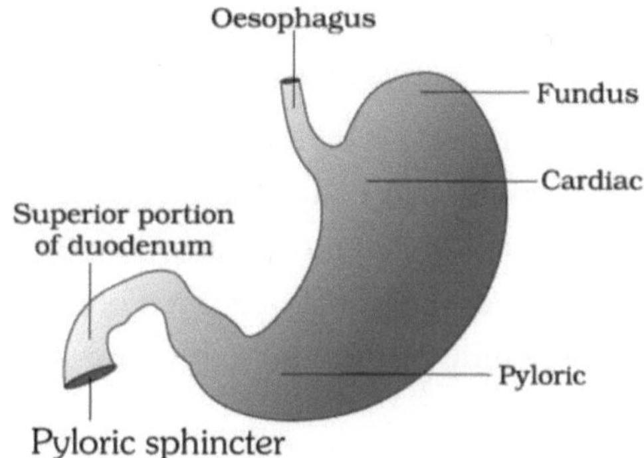

Fig. – Structure of Stomach (mammals)

Pyloric sphincter-

- It is a ring of smooth muscles and connective tissue surrounding an opening between the pyloric region of the stomach and duodenum.
- It opens and closes several times. With each opening, a small amount of food (chyme) moves into the duodenum.

Small Intestine-

- It consists of three parts.

  (a) Duodenum **(b) Jejunum** **(c) Ileum.**

(a) **Duodenum-** It form the upper part of small intestine which is C shaped and about 9 inches long and is only one inch in diameter. It gets pancreatic juice from pancreas and bile juice from liver through a common bile duct.

(b) **Jejunum-** Duodenum leads into a coiled tube called jejunum that is about 7 feet long.

(c) **Ileum-** Jejunum leads to ileum. The internal wall is thrown into number of folds called villi which increase the surface area for absorption.

Large Intestine-

It is much shorter than small intestine and is basically for absorption of water and discharging the undigested wastes. It has three parts, caecum, colon and rectum.

(a) Caecum-

- Caeum is a blind sac and is present where ileum joins the large intestine (just below the opening of ileum).
- In case of humans, it is very small and from it extends a small finger like **vermiform appendix** which gets infected during appendicitis (Fig.).
- Caecum is large and spacious and a food storage organ in herbivores where cellulose fermentation takes place.

(b) Colon-

- It may be 5-6 feet long and 3 inches in diameter and is present in the form of an inverted U in the abdominal cavity (Fig.).

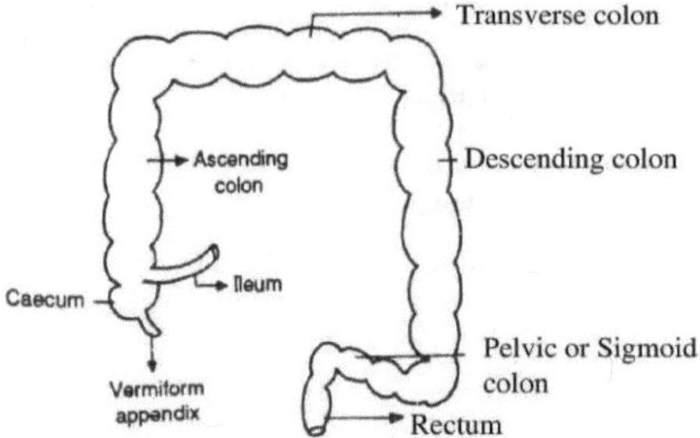

Fig.- Parts of large intestine

- **Ascending colon** is the first part present on the right side that moves upwards from the caecum.
- **Transverse colon** is the horizontal part placed transversely.
- **Descending colon** is the next region that moves down on the left side.
- **Pelvic colon-** It is S shaped and continues into rectum. Food can remain in the colon for a long time may be as long as 36 hours before being passed out to rectum.

(c) Rectum -

It is a small muscular region at the end of the large intestine. It can store the undigested food for a very short time before passing it out through anus.

2. DIGESTIVE GLANDS-

- Apart from large number of gastric and intestinal glands present in the lining of the stomach, there are three main associated digestive glands which pour their secretions into the alimentary canal.
- They are salivary glands, gastric gland, liver, pancreas and intestine gland.

I. **Salivary glands**

- There are 3 pairs of salivary glands.

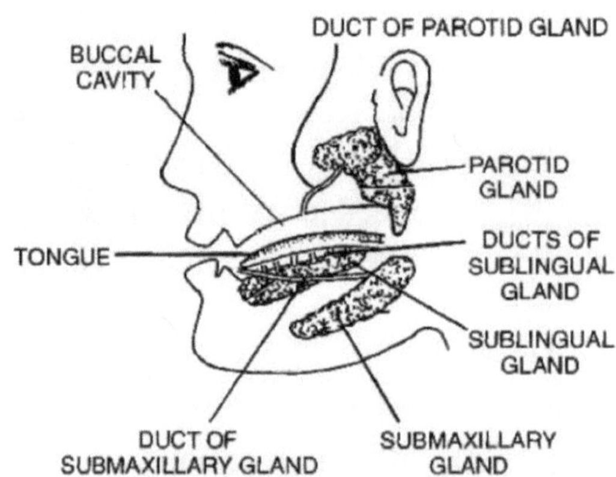

Human Salivary Glands

I. Salivary glands :

It produces saliva. In rabbit, 4 pairs of salivary glands are present while in man only three pairs of salivary glands are present. They help in chemical digestion. They secrete an enzyme called **salivary amylase** or **ptyalin**. It helps in digestion of starch.

(A) **Parotid glands :** largest glands present just below the external ear. In this glands, virus causes mumps disease. (Parotid duct/Stenson's duct)

(B) **Submaxillary glands / Submandibular glands :** These lie beneath the jaw-angles. (Wharton's duct)

(C) **Sublingual glands :** Smallest glands which lie beneath the tongue and open at the floor of buccal cavity.(Duct of Rivinus)

II. Gastric glands :

- Present in stomach. They secrete hydrochloric acid, protein digesting enzymes and mucus.
- These are of 3 types :

  (A) Cardiac glands : secrete an alkaline mucus.

  (B) Pyloric glands : secrete an alkaline mucus.

  (C) Fundic glands : each gland has 5 type of cells.

  1. Peptic / Zymogen cells : secrete pepsinogen, prorennin.

  2. Oxyntic cells : Secrete HCl

  3. Goblet cells : secrete mucus

  4. Argentaffin cells : produces serotonin somatostatin and histamine

  5. G-cells : secrete and store the hormone gastrin.

III. Liver-

- It is the **largest gland** of the body that lies in the **upper right region** of the abdomen just below the diaphragm.
- It secretes **bile** -a brownish-green fluid that passes from liver through hepatic ducts (that form of a shape) and is poured into the common bile duct that opens in the duodenum (Fig.).
- Bile contains bile pigments and organic salts called bile salts. It helps in digestion of fats.

Function of liver :

- Formation of glucose from excess organic acids.
- Storage of vitamins : A, D, E, B_{12} Synthesis of vitamin A from carotene.
- Secretions of blood anticoagulant named **heparin**.
- Synthesis of blood or plasma proteins, fibrinogen and prothrombin.
- Secretion of bile, detoxification of harmful chemicals.
- Elimination of pathogens and foreign particles through phagocytic cells called **Kupffer's cells**.
- The bile juice is secreted through common bile duct into the duodenum, but if there is no food in the intestine, it is passed to the gall bladder through cystic duct.
- The gall bladder a small sac below liver, stores and concentrates bile. During digestion it contracts to release the stored bile into the duodenum.

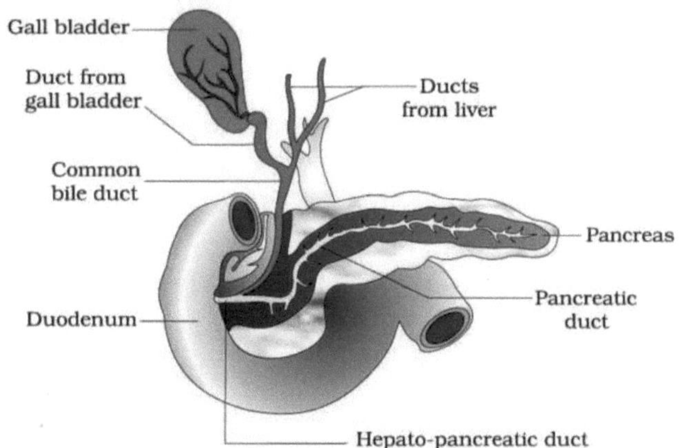

Fig. The duct systems of liver, gall bladder and pancreas

IV. Pancreas-

- It is a compound gland having dual function - exocrine as well as endocrine.
- The exocrine part secretes pancreatic juice.
- It is located in the bend of the duodenal loop.
- The pancreatic juice passes into the duodenum through pancreatic duct which joins the common bile duct.
- Pancreatic juice contains three enzymes -**(i) trypsin (ii) amylase and (iii) lipase.**

V. Intestinal glands

- Throughout the internal lining of small intestine are present numerous unicelluar glands, called **intestinal glands**, that secrete **intestinal juice or succus entericus**.
- It contains many enzymes that help in the digestion of food.

DIGESTION IN DIFFERENT PARTS OF ALIMENTARY CANAL :

1. Digestion in buccal cavity (Salivary phase of digestion)

- Digestion of food starts in the buccal cavity.
- The ingested food is masticated (chewed) in the buccal cavity with the help of grinding teeth.
- Saliva secreted by the salivary glands during mastication is mixed with the food.
- The saliva performs many functions, such as :

(i) It moistens and lubricates the internal lining of buccal cavity and tongue to facilitate swallowing and speaking.

(ii) It moistes and lubricates the food.

(iii) It helps in binding the food particles and making a food bolus that helps in swallowing.

(iv) It acts as a solvent to dissolve some food particles that stimulates taste buds and allow us to know the tastes of the food.

(v) Saliva contains two enzymes named salivary amylases (ptyalin) and maltase that help in the digestion of food as follows :

$$\text{Starch} \xrightarrow[\text{or Ptyalin}]{\text{Salivary amylase}} \text{Maltose}$$

$$\text{Maltose} \xrightarrow{\text{Maltase}} \text{Glucose}$$

Salivary enzymes act in neutral or slightly alkaline medium (pH = 7.2)

(vi) Saliva clean the mouth and also destroys bacteria to prevent tooth decay.

Swallowing

- The passage of food bolus from buccal cavity into the stomach through pharynx and oesophagus is called **swallowing**.
- The process of swallowing involves many simultaneous actions.
- The tongue is pressed against the roof of buccal cavity (palate) to provide a push to the food bolus.
- As a result of this push, food bolus reaches the pharynx, from where it passes into the oesophagus and finally into the stomach.
- Lubrication of internal lining of oesophagus facilitates the passage of food.
- During swallowing of food, its entry into the nasal chambers is prevented by the posterior part of palate.
- Similarly, food cannot enter into the wind-pipe. (larynx) because its opening is closed by the flap-like epiglottis.

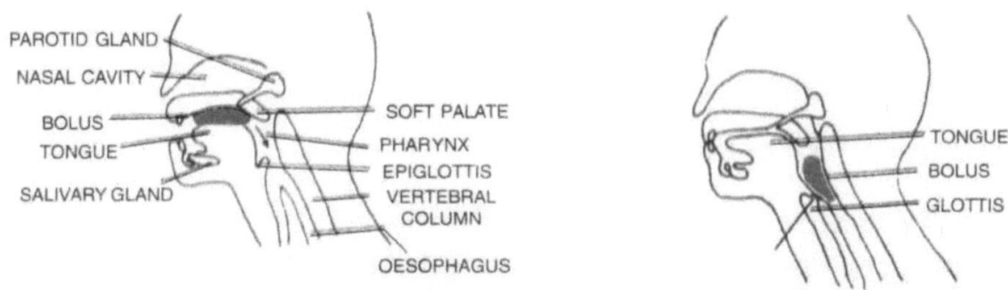

Figure : Swallowing Showing Closure of glottis by epiglottis and momentary stoppage of breathing

- In case the food enters into the windpipe due to any reason, there is spontaneous coughing which forcibly removes the food from the wind-pipe.

Peristalsis

- The process of waves of contractions in the wall of alimentary canal pushing the food forward is called **peristalsis** and the wave of contraction is called **peristaltic movement**.

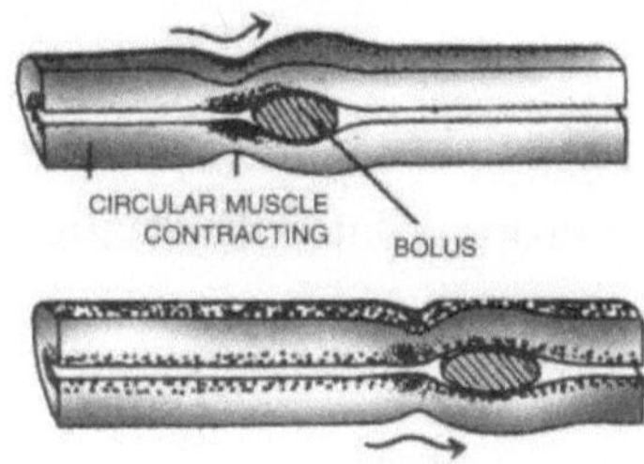

Figure : Peristaltic movement

- Food bolus keeps on rolling from its anterior to posterior side due to the peristaltic movements as shown in figure.
- Peristaltic movements occur because of the contraction of circular muscles present all along the length of alimentary canal.
- Mucus lining the internal lining of gut facilitates in the passage of food because of lubrication.

2. Digestion in stomach (Gastric phase of digestion)

- Whatever food is taken by man, reaches in the stomach and stored there for about 3 hours. To accommodate about 2-3 litres of food the elastic stomach gets disteneded.

Churning of food –

- When the stomach receives food, the highly muscular wall of stomach undergoes alternate contractions and relaxations causing the churning of food.
- Churning of food breaks large particles of food physically into smaller ones.

Partial digestion of food –

- In the stomach, the food is mixed with **gastric juice** secreted by the gastic glands.
- Gastric juice contains large quantities of mucus which when mixed with the food liquefies the food.
- HCl kills bacteria that may accompany the food.
- HCl also converts inactive enzymes **pepsinogen** and **prorennin** present in the gastric juice into their active forms.
- Various steps of digestion in the stomach can be summarised as follows :

$$\text{Prorennin} \xrightarrow{\text{HCl}} \text{Rennin}$$

$$\text{Pepsinogen} \xrightarrow{\text{HCl}} \text{Pepsin}$$

$$\text{Casein} \xrightarrow{\text{Rennin}} \text{Paracasein}$$

(Soluble milk protein) (Insoluble protein)

$$\text{Proteins} \xrightarrow{\text{Pep sin}} \text{Peptones} + \text{Proteoses}$$

- Because of churning, mixing of gastric juice and partial digestion, the food in the stomach is converted into a thick paste (pulp-like material) called **chyme**.
- The chyme enters into the small intestine in small amounts at a time.

3. Digestion in small intestine

- Digestion of food is complete in the small intestine.
- The food comes across three digestive juices in this part of the gut. These digestive juices are :

(a) Bile **(b) Pancreatic juice and** **(c) Intestinal juice**

(a) Bile :

- The important functions of bile are :

(i) It neutralizes acidity of chyme.

(ii) It prepares alkaline medium for the action of enzymes present in pancreatic and intestinal juices.

(iii) It **emulsifies** fats, i.e., breaks larger drops of fats into smaller droplets. It increases surface area for the action of enzymes.

(b) Pancreatic juice :

- It is alakline in nature and contains three types of enzymes, i.e.

(i) **Pancreatic amylase :** It digests the left over straches into maltose.

(ii) **Trypsin :** It converts peptones and proteoses into small peptides and amino acids ; and

(iii) **Lipase :** Its acts on fats and converts them into fatty acids and glycerol.

These reactions are summarized as follow :

$$\text{Starch} \xrightarrow{\text{Amylase}} \text{Maltose}$$

$$\text{Peptone and proteoses} \xrightarrow{\text{Tryspin}} \text{Peptides} + \text{Amino acids}$$

$$\text{Fats} \xrightarrow{\text{Lipase}} \text{Fatty acids} + \text{Glycerol}$$

(c) Intestinal juice :

The partially digested food now enters into the ileum where intestinal juice i.e. "Succus entericus" (Intestinal juice) is secreted. At this place digestion is completed.

- It contains many enyzmes that help in the completion of digestion of food. These enzymes are :

(i) **Maltase** which digests maltose and produces glucose.

(ii) **Lactase** converts milk sugar lactose into glucose and galactose.

(iii) **Invertase (Sucrase)** that splits sucrose into glucose and fructose and

(iv) **Lipase** which digests fats into fatty acids and glycerol.

$$\text{Maltose} \xrightarrow{\text{Maltase}} \text{Glucose}$$

$$\text{Lactose} \xrightarrow{\text{Lactase}} \text{Glucose} + \text{Galactose}$$

$$\text{Sucrose} \xrightarrow{\text{Sucrase}} \text{Glucose} + \text{Fructose}$$

$$\text{Fats} \xrightarrow{\text{Lipase}} \text{Fatty acids} + \text{Glycerol}$$

- In this way insoluble, indiffusible forms of food are converted into soluble and diffusible forms.
- This simple and diffusible food in the small intestine is present in the form of a liquid called **chyle**.
- Now digested food is absorbed from small intestine into the blood.

Summary of digestion of food in various parts of alimentary canal of man

Region		Secretion (Source gland)	Enzymes	Nutrient (Substrate)	Product of digestion
Buccal cavity		Saliva (Salivary glands)	(i) Ptyalin (Salivary amylase (ii) Maltase	Starch, Maltose	Maltose, Glucose
Oesophagus		None	–	–	–
Stomach		Gastric juice & Hydrochloric and (Gastric glands)	Pepsin Rennin (Not found in adult humans)	Proteins Milk protein or casein	Proteoses and peptones Crudling of milk, caseinogen
Small Intestine	Duodenum	Bile (Liver)	None		Emulsifies fats, food made alkaline
		Pancreatic juice Pancrease)	Pancreatic analayse Trypsin Lipase	Strach Proteins Emulsified fats	Maltose Proteoses, peptones, peptides Fatty acids and glycerol
	Ileum	Intestinal juice (Intenstinal glands between villi)	Maltase	Maltose	Glucose
			Sucrase (Invertase)	Sucrose	Glucose and frutose
			Lactase	Lactose	Glucose and galactose
			Lipase	Fats	Fatty acids & glycerol
Large Intestine	Colon	None	–	–	Absorbs water and some remnants of digested food
	Rectum	None	–	–	Temporarily stores undigested food and faeces.

ABSORPTION :

- Diffusion of digested food through the internal lining of alimentary canal into the blood is called **absorption**.
- Very little absorption takes place through the internal lining of stomach.
- Maximum absorption takes place through the internal lining of small intestine (ileum).
- To bring about efficient absorption, the small intestine contains longitudinal folds (**villi**) which increase the surface area for absorption, Moreover, in each villus there is an elaborate network of blood capillaries and an unbranched lymph vessel called **lacteal**.
- Glucose, fructose, galactose, amino acids, minerals and vitamins from the digested food diffuse through the internal lining of ileum into the blood running through capillary network of each villus.
- All the blood vessels that collect blood from alimentary canal join to form the **hepatic portal vein**.
- It carries blood along with digested food to the liver.

- Fatty acids and glycerol from the chyle diffuse into the lymph running in lacteal which finally pours it into the blood stream.

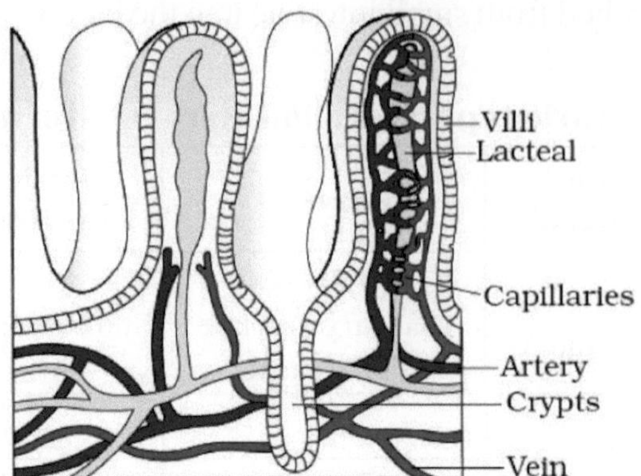

Fig. A section of small intestinal mucosa showing villi

- After the absorption of digested food the remaining part of chyle in the form of liquid reaches the large intestine.

Absorption of water in large intestine

- Almost liquid - like undigested materials pass into the large intestine.
- Water from the undigested material is absorbed into the blood through the internal lining of colon.
- The undigested material is converted into semi-solid **faeces**.
- Semi-solid faeces are pushed into the rectum fom where they are passed out of the body through the anus. The process of passing out faeces is called **egestion** or **defaecation**.

ASSIMILATION OF FOOD :

- Conversion of digested food into the living protoplasm of cells is called **assimilation**.
- Digested food is supplied to every cell by the blood stream.
- From the digested food which reaches any cell, most of the glucose is oxidized during metabolic activities.
- The remaining monosaccharides are converted into polysacharides, the amino acids are converted into proteins and fatty acid and glycerol into fats.

EGESTION

- Removal of undigested food out of the body is called **egestion** or **defaecation.**
- Undigested materials in the form of faeces are eliminated from the body.
- **Undigested food-** Which mainly consists of cellulose and other plants fibres.
- **Dead bacteria-** Intestine harbours many symbiotic bacteria which synthesise amino acids and some vitamins like vitamin K.
- **Mucus and dead mucosal cells from the gut wall-** The gut lining is constantly shed off or wears off and is replaced by new cells.
- Bile pigments and its derivatives give colour to faeces.

SOME DISEASES

1. **Peptic Ulcer:** A lesion on the inner membrane of the stomach, because of higher acidity of gastric juice.
2. **Dental Caries:** Gradual softening of enamel and dentine. Bacteria acts on sugars and produce acid which **demineralises** the enamel.

   Masses of bacterial cells together with food particles stick to the teeth to form dental plaque.

RESIRATION

Metabolism :

- The sum total of all the vital activities is called as **metabolism.**
- Vital activities refer to all the physiochemical activities of a cell.
- It has two aspects :

(i) **Anabolism :** It includes metabolic process by which complex cellular compounds are synthesized from simpler compounds, .e.g. **Photosynthesis**

(ii) **Catabolism :** It includes metabolic processes by which larger molecules are broken down into simpler molecules, e.g. **Respiration.**

- Respiration is an important catabolic process responsible for the production of energy.

Definition :

- Respiration is a multistep, enzyme mediated biochemical process of oxidative breakdown of organic compounds inside living cells releasing small packets of energy at various steps.
- It is, therefore, a catabolic and exergonic process.
- Energy liberated during oxidative breakdown of respiratory substrate is partly stored in ATP (adenosine triphosphate). The rest is dissipated as heat.

$$C_6H_{12}O_6 + 6O_2 \xrightarrow{\text{enzymes}} 6CO_2 + 6H_2O + 38\text{ATP out of 686 kcal/2870 kJ.}$$

Recent Equation :

$$C_6H_{12}O_6 + 6O_2 + 6H_2O \xrightarrow{\text{enzymes}} 6CO_2 + 12H_2O + 38\text{ATP out of 686 kcal/2870 kJ.}$$

Differences Between Respiration and combustion

	Respiration	Combustion
1. **Cellular**	It is a cellular process which occurs inside living cells.	It is a non-cellular process.
2. **Temperature**	Temperature does not rise above 40°C.	Combustion produces temperature of 600-2000°C.
3 **Control**	It is under biological control	It is an uncontrolled process.
4. **Steps**	It is a multistep reaction.	It is single step involved
5. **Enzymes**	A number of enzymes take part in reaction.	No enzyme is involed.
6. **Energy**	It is released in small packets in several steps.	It is released in large amount in one step.
7. **Heat and Light**	About 50% of energy is liberated as heat. Light is not produced.	Whole energy is produced as heat and light.
8. **Storage of Energy**	50% of liberated energy is stored as ATP molecules.	There is no storage of energy.
9. **Intermediates**	Several intermediates are produced.	No intermediates are produced.
10. **Oxidation**	It is terminal where oxygen combines with hydrogen of reduced coenzymes.	Oxidation is direct where every oxidisable atom oxidized without relation to presence of hydrogen.

ACTIVITY :–

Carbon Dioxide is produced during respiration.

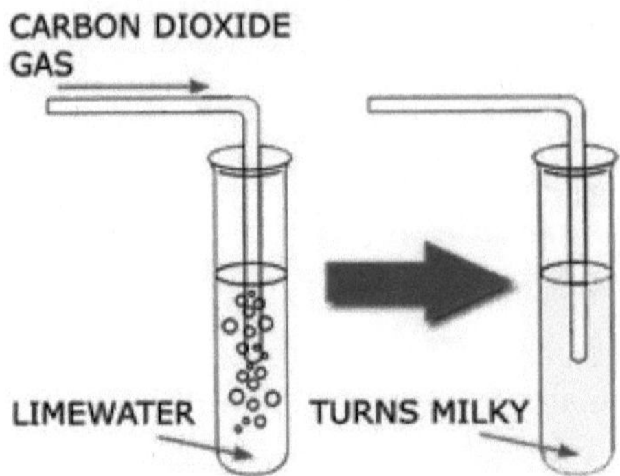

Procedure :– Pour freshly prepared lime water into a test tube upto its one third. Blow air from mouth into the lime water with the help of a glass tube. Pour a similar amount of lime water in another test tube. Blow air into it with the help of small air pump or syringe fitted with a fine rubber tubing.

Observation :– Lime water turns milky within no time when air is blown from mouth. It takes a lot of air and a long period for lime water to turn milky when fresh air is blown into it.

Inference :– Lime water turns milky only when carbon dioxide mixed with it to form calcium carbonate. Air blown from mouth is actually breathed out air. Since it turns lime water milky within no time, the exhaled air contains good concentration of carbon dioxide. It is several times more than normally present in air because fresh air blown in lime water takes a long time to turn it milky. Therefore, carbon dioxide is produced during respiration.

RESPIRATION AND PHOTOSYNTHESIS

- Respiration and photosynthesis are the two antagonistic and complementary processes in plants involving gaseous exchanges. The substrates in one process are the end-products of the other process.

$$C_6H_{12}O_6 + 6O_2 \underset{\text{Photosynthesis}}{\overset{\text{Respiration}}{\rightleftharpoons}} 6CO_2 + 6H_2O + \text{Energy}$$

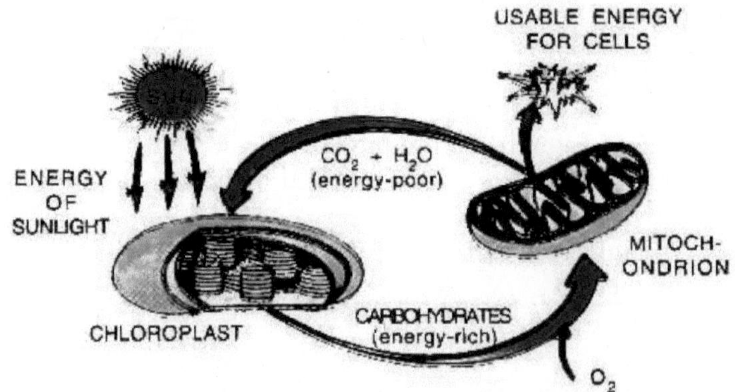

Figure : Schematic diagram to show the flow of energy in plants during photosynthesis

Differences between Photosynthesis and Respiration

Photosynthesis	Respiration
1. **Metabolism.** Photosynethesis is a synthetic or anabolic	Respiration is a breakdown or catabolic process.
2. **Energy Relation.** It is an endergonic process	It is an exergonic process.
3 **Energy Conversion.** It converts light energy into chemical energy.	It liberates chemical energy which is used as such or changed into other forms of energy.
4. **Timing.** Photosynthesis occurs during the daytime when light is available.	Respiration occurs all the time.
5. **Cells.** It occurs only in green cells.	It occurs in all types of living cells.
6. **Carbon Dioxide.** It absorbs carbon dioxide.	Respiration liberates carbon dioxide.
7. **Oxygen.** Photosynthesis liberates oxygen.	Respiration consumes oxygen.
8. **Raw Material.** They are carbon dioxide and water.	There is no storage of energy.
9. **End products.** They are glucose, other organic substances and oxygen.	End products are carbon dioxide and water.
10. **Weight.** There is net gain of weight	Oxidation is direct where every oxidisable atom oxidized without relation to presence of hydrogen.

Remember :

The low light intensity at which the rate of photosynthesis equals the rate of respiration is called **compensation point**. At this point the gas evolved in one process is just sufficient for the other process i.e. photosynthesis and respiration balance each other and there is no gaseous exchange.

RESPIRATION IN PLANTS :

- Like other living organisms, plants also exchange gases with their environment.
- However, plants do not posses any transport system for the gases.
- Different parts of plants exchange gases independently. The gases move entirely by diffusion.
- Respiration is rapid in meristematic regions (stem tips, root tips, cambia), floral buds, growing fruits and germinating seeds.
- It is slower in mature regions.

(a) Young Roots :–

- Air occurs in soil interspaces.
- Root hairs as well as epiblem cells of the young roots are in contact with them.
- They are also permeable to metabolic gases.
- Oxygen of the soil air diffuses through root hair–epiblema cells and reaches all internal cells of the young root.
- Carbon dioxide produced by root cells diffuses in the opposite direction.
- In water–logged conditions, soil air becomes deficient. In the absence of oxygen, metabolic activity of the root declines and the plant may wither.

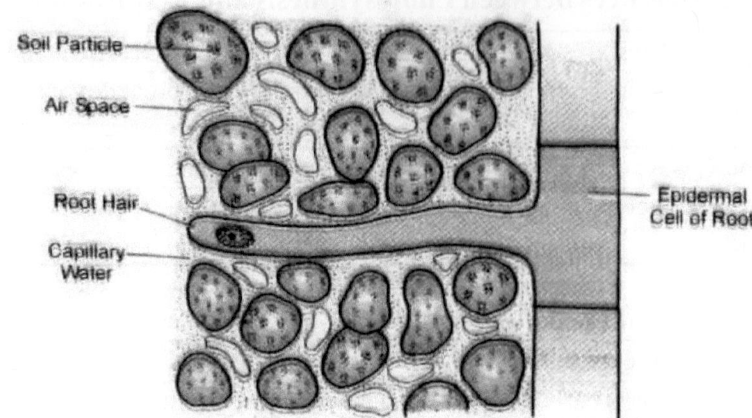

Figure : Epiblema and root hair take part in exchange of gases directly in young roots

(b) Older Roots and Stems :–

- In older roots and stems, the surface tissues are impermeable to gases.
- They have permanently open pores called lenticels.
- Each lenticel contains a mass of loosely arranged complementary cells that enclose a number of intercellular spaces.
- Exchange of gases occurs through them.

(c) Leaves and Young Stems :–

- Leaves and young stems are ideally suited to quick exchange of gases.
- The organs have a covering of nearly impermeable epidermis for reducing loss of water.
- The epidermis bears a number of aerating pores called **stomata**.

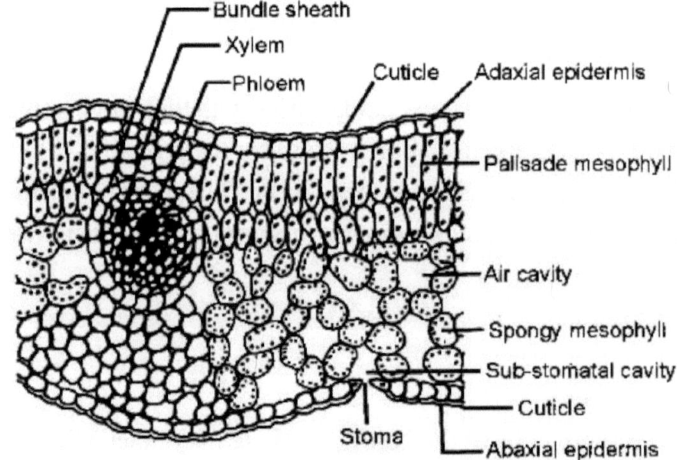

Figure : Section of leaf to show intercellular spaces and stomata.

- Each aerating or stomatal pore is bordered by a pair of guard cells.
- In most of the plants, the guard cells are kidney or bean shaped with inner walls being thicker and less elastic then the outer walls.
- Guard cells contain chloroplasts which are absent in other epidermal cells.
- Opening and closing of stomata are regulated.

RESPIRATION IN ANIMALS :

Respiratory organs :–

- Various animals possess different organs for the exchange of gases. (Except endoparasites, such as, Taenia (tape worm), Ascaris, etc. which respire anaerobically, most of the animals respire aerobically.)
- These respiratory organs found in different animals are designed to suit their habitat.
- The following organs act as respiratory organs in different animals.

(a) General body surface :

- In lower organisms, such as, protists, sponges, cnidarians (**Protozoa, *Hydra*, Planaria, etc.**) exchange of gases occurs through the body surface via the cell membrane by simple diffusion.

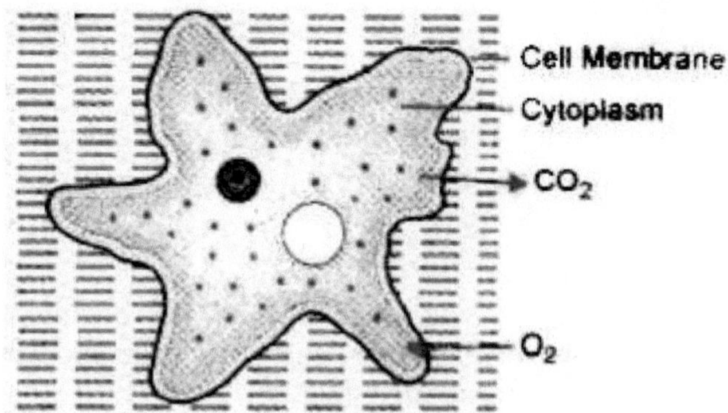

Figure : Cell surface exchange of gases in Amoeba

(b) Skin or body surface :

- The skin or general body surface or epidermis acts as respiratory organ in some animals, such as, **annelids** and **amphibian** that live in semiaquatic habitat.
- This type of respiration in which exchange of gases occurs through the skin is called cutaneous respiration.

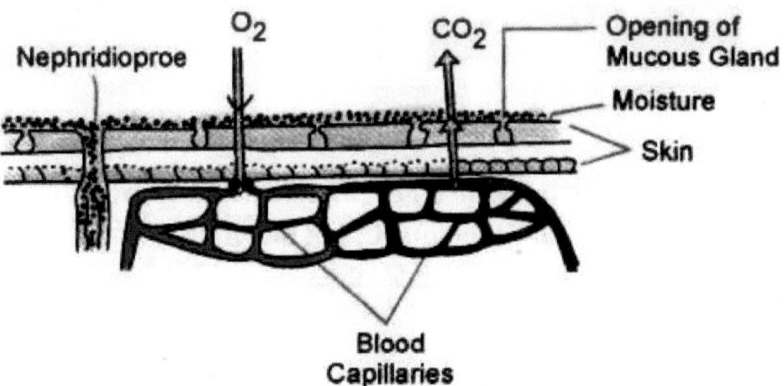

Figure : Cutaneous exchange of gases in Earthworm

(c) Tracheae (air tubes) :

- Terrestrial arthropods, such as, **insects**, **millipedes** and **centipedes** have thick impermeable integument to minimize loss of water from their body surface by evaporation.
- They have evolved a complex system of whitish, shining, intercommunicating air tubes called **tracheae**.
- The exchange of gases with the help of tracheae is termed **tracheal respiration**.

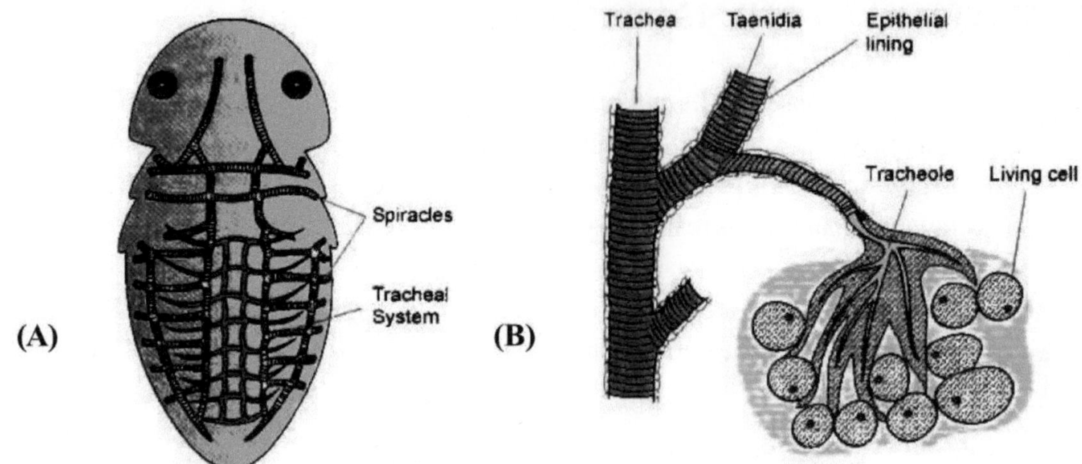

Figure : Tracheal respiratoty system in Cockroach.
A. Tracheal system. B. Branches of trachea

Gills :–

- Aquatic animals, such as, prawns, mussels, fishes and tadpoles, breathe water.
- They draw oxygen dissolved in water and release carbon dioxide into water.
- The organs used for breathing water are called **gills**.
- The exchange of gases in the gills is known as **branchial respiration**.

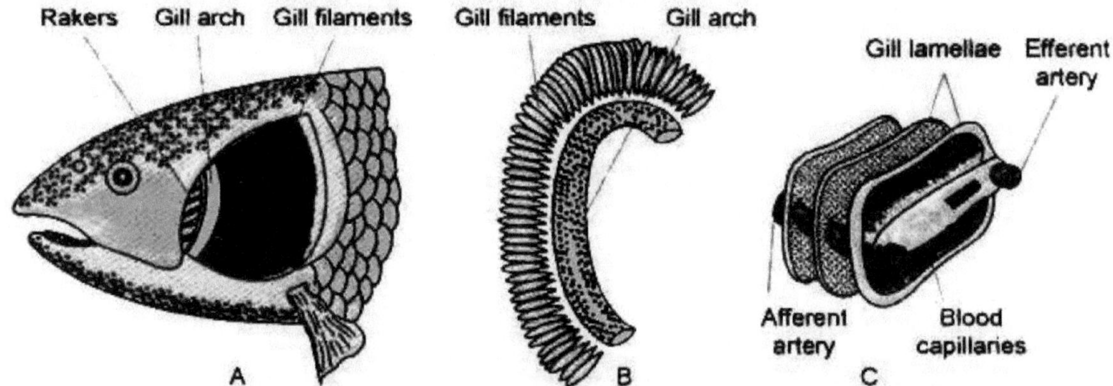

Figure : Gill respiration in Fish. A. gill chamber with operculum removed.
B. gill filaments. C. gill lamellae.

Activity :

Study of Branchial Respiration in Fish

Observe a fish in the aquarium. Find out that it is regularly opening and closing its mouth as well as operculum. Place a few small crystals of potassium permanganate carefully in front of the mouth of a fish. They enter the mouth of the fish. Coloured water is observed to come out from the lower part of operculum indicating that water regularly enters the mouth, passes into gill chambers and comes out through opening of operculum.

In gill chambers exchange of gases occurs between water and blood capillaries contained in gill lamellae. Count the number of times the fish opens and closes its mouth per minute. Compare it with your breathing rate. It is very rapid because water has low oxygen content than the content of oxygen present in air.

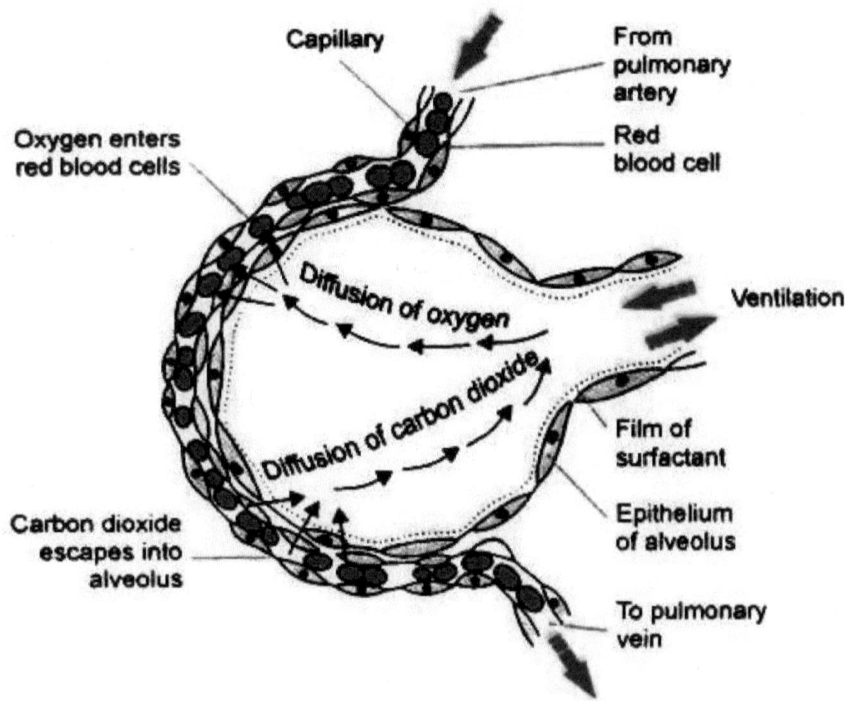

Figure : Exchange of gases in alveolus.

LUNGS

- Land animals, namely, reptiles, birds and mammals breathe atmospheric air with lungs.
- Their skin is not respiratory because it is impermeable to minimise the loss of water by evaporation.
- The amphibians also have lungs for pulmonary respiration. But, they have cutaneous respiration too with their permeable skin.
- Amphibians and reptiles have sac-like lungs with small infoldings that increases surface area for gas exchange.
- Birds and mammals have spongy lungs, consisting of millions of microscopic, capillary-surrounding air sacs. This maximizes the respiratory surface.
- Depending upon the oxidation of food in the presence or absence of oxygen, respiration is of two types:
  1. **Aerobic respiration**
  2. **Anaerobic respiration**
- Both types of respiration have a common pathway called glycolysis.
- Glycolysis does not need oxygen and takes place in the cytoplasm.
- During glycolysis, the glucose molecule is broken down to 2 molecules of pyruvic acid.
- Further breakdown of pyruvic acid depends on the presence or absence of oxygen.
- In the presence of oxygen (aerobic respiration), the pyruvic acid enters the Kreb's cycle and is broken down to carbon dioxide and water.
- In the absence of oxygen (anaerobic respiration), pyruvic acid is broken down to ethyl alcohol or lactic acid.

1. Anaerobic Respiration

- Anaerobic respiration occurs in the absence of oxygen and is catalysed by enzymes present in the cytoplasm.

- It results in incomplete oxidation of food (glucose).
- It takes place in lower organisms like yeast, certain bacteria and fungi.
- It also occurs in higher plants and animals under certain conditions, when O_2 is limiting.
- In humans, during vigorous muscular exercise, when the demand of O_2 is more than what is supplied by respiration, muscle cells start respiring anaerobically temporarily.
- It is less efficient than aerobic respiration as only 2 ATP molecules are released from one glucose molecule.
- During anaerobic respiration, glucose is first broken down to 2 molecules of pyruvic acid by glycolysis.
- Further breakdown of pyruvic acid continues but differs in plants and animals as they contain different enzymes.

a. In yeast, bacteria (microbes) and plants, pyruvic acid is broken down to ethyl alcohol and carbon dioxide is released. In these, anaerobic respiration is also known as fermentation.

$$\underset{\text{(glucose)}}{C_6H_{12}O_6} \longrightarrow \underset{\text{(Ethyl acohol)}}{2C_2H_5OH} + \underset{\text{(Carbon dioxide)}}{2CO_2} + \underset{\text{(2 ATP)}}{\text{Energy}}$$

b. In animals, pyruvic acid is broken down to lactic acid.

$$\underset{\text{(Glucose)}}{C_6H_{12}O_6} \longrightarrow \underset{\text{(Lactic acid)}}{2C_3H_6O_3} + \underset{\text{(2 ATP)}}{\text{Energy}}$$

- The lactic acid produced accumulates in the muscles and causes muscle fatigue. During resting period, when oxygen becomes available, slowly lactic acid is removed from the muscles.

2. Aerobic Respiration

- Aerobic respiration needs the presence of oxygen and occurs in mitochondria.
- The food (glucose) is completely broken down to carbon dioxide (CO_2) and water (H_2O).
- It occurs in all higher organisms (both plants and animals).
- It is highly efficient in comparison to anaerobic respiration and releases 38 ATP molecules from one glucose molecule.
- Aerobic respiration is completed in two major phases given below:

A. Anaerobic phase or glycolysis :

- It is the first phase and does not require oxygen.
- It takes place in the cytoplasm.
- The glucose molecule is broken down to 2 molecules of pyruvic acid.

B. Aerobic phase :

- It is the second phase that takes place in the presence of oxygen.
- It takes place in mitochondria.
- The pyruvic acid molecules formed during glycolysis are completely broken down to carbon dioxide and water.
- It is also called as **Krebs cycle.**

An overall equation of aerobic respiration :

$$\textbf{Glucose} \xrightarrow[\substack{\text{(No oxygen is required)} \\ \text{(in cytoplasm)}}]{\text{Glycolysis}} \textbf{Pyruvic acid} \xrightarrow[\substack{O_2 \\ \text{(in mitochondria)}}]{\text{Krebs cycle}} \textbf{Carbon dioxide + Water + Energy}$$

RESPIRATORY SYSTEM OF MAN

- All the organs in an animals that provide free O_2 and help in the removal of CO_2 collectively constitute the **respiratory system**. When the respiratory organs are lungs, it is called **pulmonary respiration**.
- In man pulmonary respiration is present. The respiration in man and other animals having pulmonary respiration can be studied in two parts :

  1. Respiratory tract **2. Respiratory organs**

1. RESPIRATORY TRACT

- The path through which O_2 reaches up to the lungs and CO_2 is removed from the lungs is called **respiratory tract**. In man it consists of :

  (a) Nose, (b) Pharynx, (c) Larynx, (d) Trachea (e) Bronchi.

(a) **The Nose :–** It consists of two nostrils which are lined with hair and mucous to filter dust and other small particles.

Do you know :

Nose breathing is better than mouth breathing as in the nose occurs

(i) filtration of air by the hair. The dust particles and other large particles are not allowed to enter the lungs.

(ii) Sterilization of air by trapping the bacteria and other pathogens in mucus.

(iii) Moistening of air by the addition of mucus and

(iv) Warming of air radiating heat.

(b) **The Pharynx :–** The nose opens into the pharynx which leads into two tubes, i.e., larynx and oesophagus, through **glottis** and **gullet** respectively. The glottis is guarded by a flaplike **epiglottis**. It does not allow anything other than air to enter into the larynx.

Pharynx serves as a common path both for the air and food.

(c) **The larynx (Voice box) :** It is the upper slightly swollen part of trachea or wind pipe. It is more prominent in men as compared to women and is called "Adam's apple". In the larynx is present a pair of vocal cords which help in the production of sound. Hence, it is also called voice box. During swallowing of food or liquid, the larynx moves upwards, so that its opening – glottis is closed by epiglottis and food does not enter into the larynx.

(d) **The trachea :** The trachea or wind pipe is a long, narrow, whitish tube. It extends through the neck. It enters the thorax where it divides into a pair of branches called **primary bronchi**. The walls of trachea are supported by "C"-shaped cartilagenous rings that keep it always distended.

(e) **The primary bronchi :** These are a pair of tubular structures formed as a result of bifurcation of the trachea. These are right and left primary bronchi that enter into the corresponding lung. These are also supported by cartilagenous rings.

2. RESPIRATORY ORGANS :

The Lungs :

- The respiratory organs in man are a pair of lungs.
- These are thin walled, elastic, spongy, pinkish, triangular and highly distensible structures known as left and right lungs.

- The lungs occupy most of the thoracic cavity.
- They are well protected by bony thoracic cage.
- Each lung is enclosed in a double–walled pleural sac.
- In between the two layers is present a fluid called **pleural fluid**.

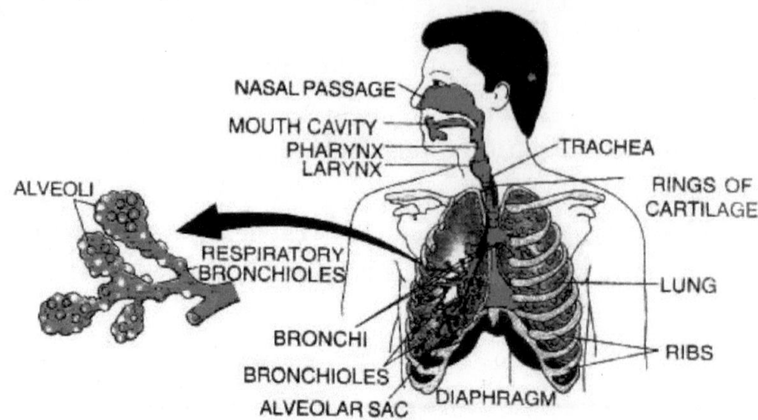

Figure. Human respiratory system.

- The pleural fluid is secreted by the pleural sac and performs the following functions:
  (i) It protects the lungs from any kind of mechanical injury and shock.
  (ii) It lubricates the lungs for free expansion and relaxation.
  (iii) It keeps the lungs moist for proper functioning.
- Each lung is a conical triangular structure.
- The upper pointed side is called apex and the lower broad side is called base.
- The left lung is slightly smaller than the right lung.
- The left lung is differentiated into two lobes with the help of furrows.
- Each primary bronchus, after entering into the corresponding lung, divides repeatedly to form a network of very fine tubes.
- The primary bronchus divides into **secondary bronchi** that give rise to **tertiary bronchi**.
- The tertiary bronchi divide into bronchioles which give rise to alveolar ducts that open into blind end sacs called **alveoli**.

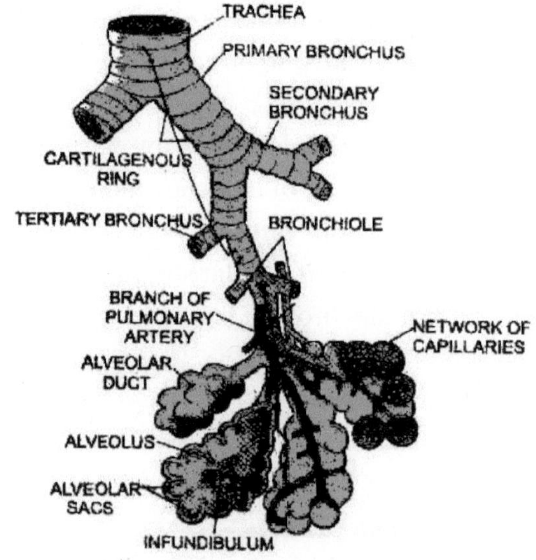

Figure. Branching of bronchion the lungs.

PHYSIOLOGY OF RESPIRATION :

- The process of respiration is a complex and continuous process. It is completed in four steps :
  (1) Breathing (2) External respiration
  (3) Internal or tissue respiration, and (4) Cellular respiration.

1. Breathing :

- Have you felt that your thorax alternately expands and contracts.
- When it is expanding you are drawing fresh air into the lungs and when it is becoming normal, you are releasing foul air from lungs.
- This movement of fresh air from outside into the lungs through respiratory tract and foul air in the opposite direction is called breathing.
- The process of breathing is an apparent and mechanical part of respiration.

Mechanism of breathing :

- Breathing is brought about by changing the volume of thoracic cavity, where lungs are present.
- The mechanism of breathing can be studied in two steps :
  (a) Inspiration (Inhalation) and
  (b) Expiration (Exhalation)

(a) Inspiration or (Inhalation)

Movement of fresh air into the lungs is called inspiration. During inspiration volume of the thoracic cavity is increased by the combined movements of sternum, ribs and diaphragm. The sternum and ribs move upwards, forwards and outwards.

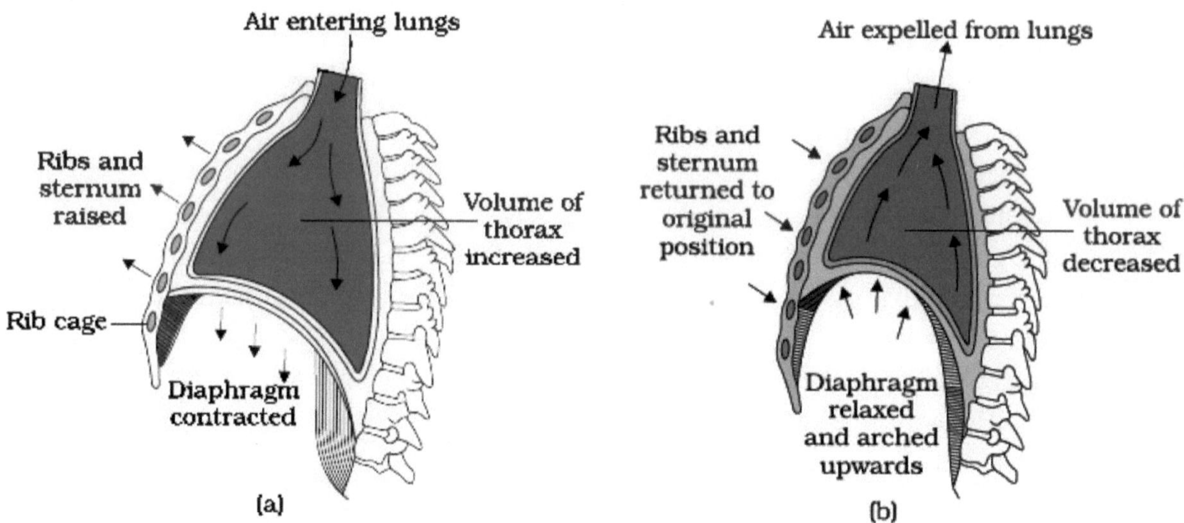

Figure. Process of breathing in man.

- Expansion of the thoracic cavity results in the expansion of lungs.
- Due to the increase in the volume of lungs pressure inside decreases as compared to the atmospheric pressure.
- Therefore, fresh atmospheric air, which is at higher pressure, rushes into the lungs through the respiratory tract to equalize the pressure.
- Exchange of O_2 and CO_2 will take place between the alveoli and blood. Now the lungs will be full of foul air.

(b) Expiration (or Exhalation)

- The movement of foul air from the lungs to outside is called expiration or exhalation.
- During expiration volume of the thoracic cavity is decreased by the inward and downward movements of the ribs and sternum and by upward bulging of the diaphragm.
- All these movements are brought about by the simple relaxation of muscles that were contracted during inspiration.
- An adult man breathes 12–14 times per minute at rest.

Do you know

- If diffusion were to move oxygen in our body, it is estimated that it would take 3 years for a molecule of oxygen to get to our toes from our lungs. Aren't you glad that we have haemoglobin?
- Process of breathing and swallowing of food cannot go together.
- Rate of breathing is minimum when a person is sleeping.
- Painful breathing is called **dyspnoea**.
- Cessation of breathing is called **apnoea**.
- Normal comfortable breathing is called **eupnoea**.
- In the lungs of man are present 750 million alveoli.
- Total surface area of the alveoli is about 100 m^2 which is 50 times more than the external surface area.

2. External respiration :

- **Exchange of O_2 and CO_2 between the inhaled air and blood through the surface of respiratory organ is called external respiration.**
- Exchange of gases takes place because of higher partial pressure of O_2 in the inhaled air and that of CO_2 in the blood supplied to the lungs.
- As a result O_2 diffuses into the blood from the alveoli of lungs and CO_2 in the opposite direction.
- Exchange of gases always takes place in the solution form. That is why, surface of respiratory organ is always kept moist.

Transportation of O_2 :

- The O_2 that diffuses into the blood from the lungs is transported to various body tissues in the following form :

(i) About 97% of the O_2 that diffuses into the blood combines with haemoglobin of RBCs forming an unstable compound, oxyhaemoglobin.

(ii) The remaining 3% O_2 dissolves into water of plasma.

3. Internal or Tissue respiration :

- Exchange of O_2 and CO_2 between the blood and body tissues is called **internal** or **tissue respiration**.
- The O_2 form the blood diffuses into the body tissues whereas CO_2 from tissues to the blood because of higher concentration of CO_2 in the body tissues, produced due to cellular respiration.

4. Cellular Respiration :

- As this process is at cellular level so it is called **cellular respiration**.
- As this process is at cellular level so it is called cellular respiration.

- It takes place in three steps :
- It refers to the oxidation of food taking place inside the cell.
- It takes place in three in 3 steps :

(i) Glycolysis **(ii) Krebs Cycle** **(iii) Electron Transport System**

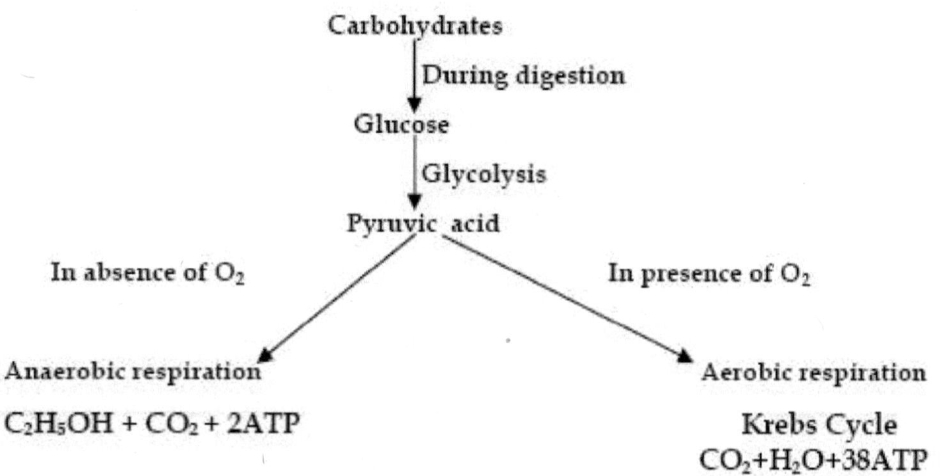

$C_2H_5OH + CO_2 + 2ATP$

Krebs Cycle
$CO_2 + H_2O + 38ATP$

(i) Glycolysis :

- Glycolysis also called **EMP (Embden Meyerhof Parnas)** pathway , site-cytoplasm of cell.

(i) In this cycle glucose is converted into pyruvic acid in presence of many enzymes and co-enzymes.
(ii) Oxygen in not required during glycolysis.
(iii) 1 molecule of glucose gives rise to 2 molecules of pyruvic acid.
(iv) In this process 4 molecules of ATP are formed among them 2ATP molecules are utilized thus net gain of ATP is two molecules.
(v) 2NAD molecules are reduced to $2NADPH_2$, which later produces 6ATP molecules.
(vi) Overall production of ATP in glycolysis is 2ATP + 6ATP = 8ATP
(vii) There is no production of CO_2 during this process.

NOTE : After glycolysis, pyruvic acid is converted into acetyl Co-A with the release of CO_2 and the process is called as **'oxidative decarboxylation'**. It occurs in mitochondria of the cell. Besides this 6ATP are also formed during this step.

(ii) Krebs Cycle :

Site : Mitochondria of cell

(i) Also called aerobic oxidation.
(ii) Discovered by Sir Hans Kreb.
(iii) Another name TCA cycle (tricarboxylic acid cycle) or Citric acid cycle.
(iv) It brings about the conversion of pyruvic acid, fatty acids, fats and amino acids into CO_2 and water by oxidation.
(v) It is the common path for oxidation of carbohydrates, fats, proteins.
(vi) It accounts for 24ATP molecules.
(vii) It starts with acetyl Co-A which is then converted into several intermediate compounds with the release of $NADPH_2$, $FADH_2$, ATP, hydrogen atoms and then Acetyl Co-A is regenerated back.

(iii) Electron Transport System or ETS :

- In this hydrogen atoms produced during oxidation of various intermediates during Kreb cycle are first broken into protons and electrons.
- These protons and electrons after passing through a series of coenzymes and cytochromes combine with oxygen to form water molecules.
- During these series of events 1NADPH$_2$ releases 3ATP molecules and 1FADH$_2$ gives 2ATP molecules which were produces during kreb cycle and glycolysis.

***Do you know* :**

The net gain of ATP molecules during respiration in 38ATP molecules among them,
8ATP from glycolysis
6ATP from conversion of pyruvic acid into acetyl CO. A
24ATP from kreb cycle
besides this CO_2 and H_2O are also released.

MECHANISM OF GASEOUS EXCHANGE BETWEEN TISSUES AND BLOOD :

- When the air enters into the lungs through nostrils, trachea and bronchi it enters into the bronchioles, from bronchioles it moves into thin walled alveolar sacs or alveoli.
- Alveoli are rich in blood capillaries, at this place oxygen from air diffuses into the blood and reaches to all the cells and tissues of body this oxygen now diffuses into the cell and is utilized for the oxidation of food and production of energy in mitochondria as a result of this carbon dioxide is produced in cells, due to this increased concentration of CO_2, it diffuses into the blood and is brought back to alveoli and expelled out of the lungs through trachea and nostrils.

Control of Respiration :

- Respiration is controlled by the respiratory centre situated in medulla oblongata of brain.

(i) Breathing occurs involuntarily.

(ii) Under normal conditions rate of breathing is 12-14 times per minute. During vigorous exercise the demand for oxygen increases due to which rate of breathing increases by about 20-25 times.

(iii) The total area for gas exchange covered through 300 million alveoli is about 36-72 m^2 in each lung.

(iv) Respiratory quotient : It is defined as the ratio of the volumes of CO_2 liberated and O_2 used during respiration.

Some Respiratory Disorders :

- **Emphysema :** It occurs due to infection, smoking etc. It occurs due to obstructions in bronchioles caused by breaking of alveolar septa. Bronchodilator and O_2 therapy are used, for curing this disease.
- **Asthma :** Air passages are narrowed and lead to obstruction in breathing.
- **Pneumonia :** Lymph and mucous accumulate in alveoli and bronchioles. It occurs due to bacterial and viral infection.
- **Bronchitis :** Swelling in living membranes of respiratory tract due to excessive smoking.
- **Tuberculosis :** Bacterial infection in lungs.
- **Pleurisy :** Inflammation of lung membrane called as **pleurisy**.
- Sudden contraction of diaphragm along with loud closure of glottis causes Hiccough.
- Sudden and violent expulsion of air through mouth and nose is called a sneezing.

Difference Between Aerobic and Anaerobic Respiration

	Aerobic Respiration	Anaerobic Respiration
1.	**Method.** It is the common method of respiration (Inhale and exhale).	It occurs permanently only in a few organism. In others it may occur as a temporary measure to overcome shortage of oxygen.
2.	**Steps.** It is completed in 3 steps – glycolysis, Krebs cycle and terminal oxidation.	There are two steps – glycolysis and anaerobic breakdown of pyruvic acid.
3.	**Oxygen.** It requires oxygen.	Oxygen is not required.
4.	**Breakdown.** Respiratory substrate is completely broken down.	Respiratory substrate is incompletely broken down.
5.	**End Products.** They are inorganic.	Atleast one end product is organic. Inorganic products may or may not be present.
6.	**Toxicity.** End products show little toxicity.	The organic end product is generally toxic.
7.	**Occurance.** It occurs partly in cytoplasm and partly in mitochondria.	Anaerobic respiration is carried out entirely in cytoplasm. Mitochondria are not required.
8.	**E.T.C.** An electron transport chain is required.	ETC is not required.
9.	**Energy.** In release 686 kcal or 2870 kJ of energy per mole of glucose.	Energy liberated is 36-50 kcal or 150-210 kJ per mole of glucose.
10.	ATP. The liberated energy issued in forming 36-38 ATP molecule per mole of glucose.	The liberate energy is used in synthesis of 2ATP mole.

CIRCULATION AND TRANSPORTATION

- The circulatory system may differ in various animals but carries out the same basic functions.

1. **Transport of nutrients. :-** It transports all the soluble food compounds from the area of absorption (like intestine in man) to different parts of the body for storage, assimilation or synthesis of new components.
2. **Transport of waste products :-** It transports all the excretory products produced as a result of cellular activities from all over the body to the organs of excretion (like kidney in mammals).
3. **Transport of intermediate metabolites :-** It transports all the by products or intermediate products from the tissue they are produced to the organ where they can be fully metabolised (like lactic acid produced in muscles is transported to liver for oxidation).
4. **Transport of hormones :-** Since hormones are produced by ductless endocrine glands, they are transported through the circulating fluid to their target organs.
5. **Uniform distribution of heat :-** Since circulatory fluid connects all parts of the body it picks up heat from one part and disspates it on the surface bringing about the uniform distribution.
6. **Transport of water, inorganic ions and various chemicals** is also done by circulating fluid so as to maintain a uniform distribution.
7. **Defence against diseases :-** The circulating fluid contains phagocytes which engulf and digest bacteria and play an important role in defending the body against disease.
8. **Transport of respiratory gases :-** In some animals the circulatory fluid contains respiratory pigments which may be dissolved in plasma like in snails, crustaceans or cephalopods or present in cells like in all vertebrates including man. The O_2 is transported from respiratory organs to tissus while CO_2 is carried from tissues to respiratory organs. Some animals like insects have a tracheal system for respiration and circulating system is not directly associated with respiration. More so it lacks any respiratory pigments.

CLOSED CIRCULATORY SYSTEM IN VERTEBRATES

- Vertebrates have a highly specialised closed circulatory system that consists of blood vessels - arteries, arterioles, capillaries, venules and veins containing blood and heart that pumps blood and drives it rapidly into the blood vessels.
- Vertebrates also have lymphatic system which helps in the activities of blood vascular system.
- There are two circulatory systems in humans:
  (i) **Blood circulatory system**
  (ii) **Lymphatic circulatory system**

Blood Circulatory System in Human Beings

It comprises –

- Blood
- Blood Vessels
- Heart or Pumping organ

BLOOD

- Blood is fluid connective tissue which comprises of

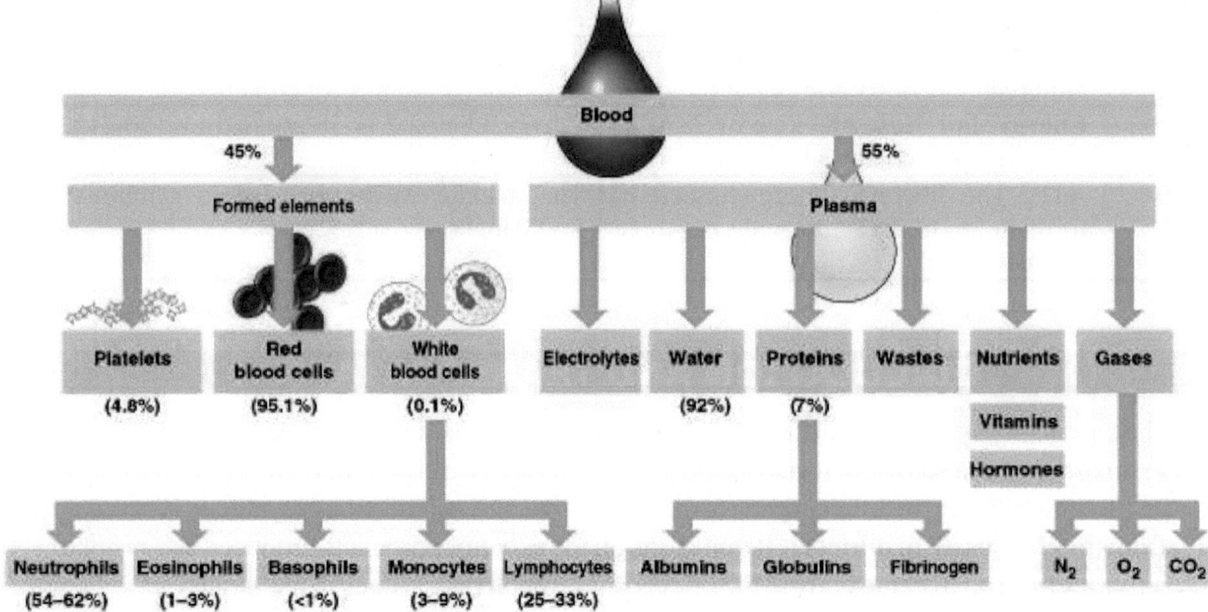

Plasma Cells

- Fluid part of blood in which corpuscles or cells are suspended.
- It contains water and dissolved substances such as proteins, nutrients, nitrogenous waste etc.
- Plasma transport food, carbon dioxide and nitrogenous waste in dissolved form.
- **Blood contains:**
  1. **Erythrocytes/RBC** (Red Blood Cell) having iron containing pigment haemoglobin for transport of oxygen to various parts of body as oxyhaemoglobin.
  2. **Leukocytes/WBC** or white blood cell helps in fighting against infections by showing phagocytosis and producing antibodies against germs. So, WBCs are called **natural soldiers of human body.**
  3. **Platelets** or blood dust are cell fragments that helps in blood clotting.

KNOW MORE

Mature RBC (Erythrocytes) lacks nucleus and other organelles in mammals.

Table : Blood Transfusion				
Blood Group	Antigen Present on RBC	Antibody present in Plasma	Can donate to blood type	Can Receive blood type
A	A	B	A and AB	A and O
B	B	A	B and AB	B and O
AB	A and B	None	AB only	All (A, B, AB and O)
O	None	A and B	All (A, B, AB and O)	O only

- Rh factor is discovered by Landsteiner & Veiner in 1940 in Rhesus monkey.
- No natural Rh antibodies are found in blood of man but if Rh^+ blood is mixed with Rh^- blood then antibodies formation starts i.e. antibodies against Rh antigens are produced in Rh^- blood.
- Marriage of Rh^+ man & Rh^- women is prohibited because due to this first birth is safe while second is fatal. This disease is called **erythroblastosis foetalis.**
- Nowadays IgG preparation is given to each Rh^- women after 1st birth for prevention.

Blood Vessels

1. Types of blood vessels :-

- As the oxygenated blood is pumped by muscular heart, it flows through arteries which are thick walled.
- Arteries branch out into arterioles and then capillaries. From capillaries the deoxygenated blood flows through venules, then to veins and is finally poured back into the heart.

Arteries

- Each artery consists of three layers. Outermost layer is made up of collagen fibres, middle layer of smooth muscles and elastic fibres and an inner layer of squamous epithelium.
- Walls of arteries are thick and elastic so as to withstand the high pressure of blood coming from heart. Because of their elasticity they can stretch and expand.
- Arteries which are further away from heart have a thicker layer of smooth muscles in the middle layer and are innervated by nerves from sympathetic nervous system so as to regulate their diameter.
- Arteries receive blood directly from heart and larger arteries branch repeatedly into smaller arteries and then to arterioles.

Arterioles

- Arteries branch further to form smaller vessels called arteriole.
- They have only smooth muscle fibres in their middle layer, innervated by sympathetic nervous system.
- On stimulation, the contraction and relaxation of these muscles can alter their diameter and hence can decrease or increase the blood flow through a particular organ.
- Arterioles branch further into a capillary network.

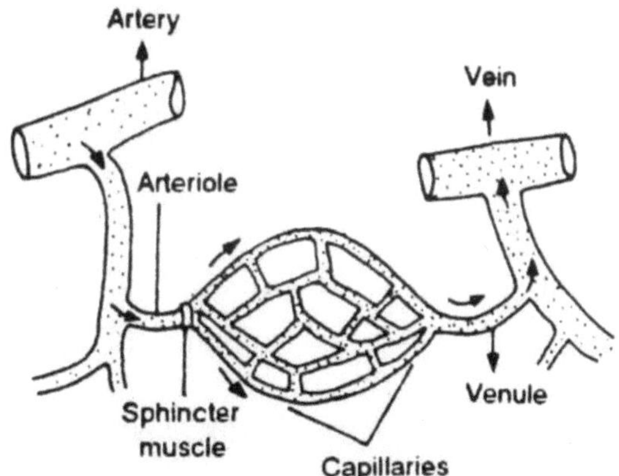

Fig.- Various blood vessels and direction of flow of blood between them

Capillaries.

- They are numerous and smallest of the blood vessels. Each capillary is about 7-10 μm in diameter.
- They are extremely thin walled and the wall consists of only a layer of endothelium
- The endothelium is very permeable and allows diffusion of dissolved substances in and out of capillaries. It does not allow macromolecules and plasma proteins to pass out of the capillaries.
- *Sphincter muscles* may be present at the points where capillaries arise from the arterioles. They contract and relax thereby regulating the decreased or increased flow of blood through capillaries.

Venules

- After exchange of materials in tissues and organs, the capillaries join together to form venules.
- The pressure in venules is very less. They collect the blood and pass it on to veins.

Veins

- Like arteries, the veins also have three layers of tissues. They have much thinner **walls** than arteries. They have less of muscle and elastic tissue in the middle layer.
- Their lumen (inner diameter through .which blood flows) is far greater than arteries
- They have semilunar **valves** (Fig.) which allow the blood to flow in one direction only i.e towards the heart. The valves prevent the back flow of blood.
- In certain parts (arms and legs) the contractions of skeletal muscles around the veins help to push the blood towards heart.
- Veins (except pulmonary vein) pour the deoxy-genated blood into the heart.

Table : Comparison of Arteries, Veins and Capillaries

		Artery	Vein	Capillary
(i)	**Cross section**	Tunica externa (Collagen fibres); Tunica media (Smooth muscles and elastic tissue); Tunica interna (Endothelium); Lumen	Tunica externa (Collagen fibres); Tunica media (Smooth muscles and elastic tissue); Tunica interna (Endothelium); Lumen	Lumen; Endothelium
(ii)	**Tunica media**	Muscle layer is thick and elastic	Muscle layer is thin, with few smooth muscles and much less elastic tissue.	Tunica media is absent. Only one layer of squamos epithelium called endothelium is present.
(iii)	**Lumen**	Small	Big	Very small
(iv)	**Semilunar Valves**	Absent	Present all along the length to prevent back flow of blood.	Absent
(v)	**Direction of**	Take the blood away from heart.	Take the blood towards the heart.	Blood flows from arterioles to venules.
(vi)	**Blood pressure**	Pressure is high and pulsative.	Pressure is low and non-pulsative.	Pressure is extremely low and non-pulsative.
(vii)	**Blood flow**	Blood flows rapidly with jerks.	Blood flows smoothly without jerks.	Blood flows smoothly without jerks.
(viii)	**Kind of blood**	Oxygenated blood except in pulmonary artery.	Deoxygenated blood except in pulmonary vein.	Blood changes from oxygenated to deoxygenated.
(ix)	**Location**	Mostly deep seated	Mostly superficial	Form a net work all over the body and in the organs.

HEART

Heart is muscular involuntary organ, which is as big as our fist. It is made up of cardiac muscles which work rhythmically. Heart is situated in middle of chest cavity but it is tilted towards left. Heart is divided into chambers. Number of chambers varies in different animals:

Fishes	-	**2 chambered heart (1 auricle, 1 ventricle)**
Amphibian & most reptiles	-	**3 chambered heart (2 auricles, 1 ventricle)**
Birds and mammals	-	**4 chambered heart (2 auricles, 2 ventricles)**

Note : (Crocodile - 3 and half chambered heart)

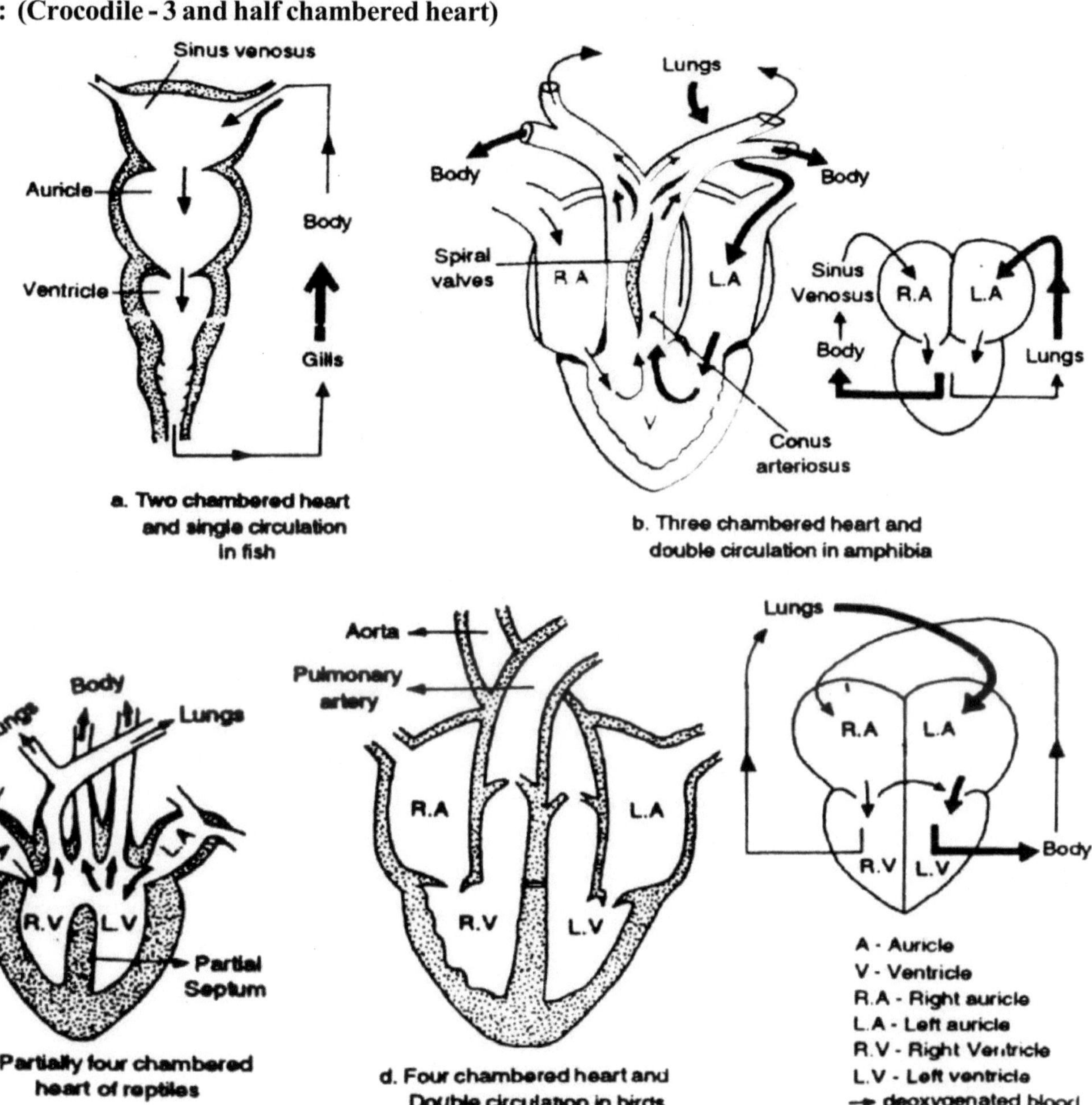

Fig. Kinds of Heat and Circulation in Vertebrates

- **Structure of Heart:** Blood circulatory system → discovered by William Harvey.
- Outer covering pericardium
- External structure

  Upper two chambers - auricles.

  lower two chambers - ventricles.

- Auricles and ventricles are separated by atria ventricular sulcus.
- Atria / auricles are separated by inter auricular septum. Left atrium is smaller than right atrium.
- Superior vena cava, inferior vena cava, coronary sinus open into right atrium.
- Superior vena cava collect blood from upper body part, inferior vena cava collects blood from lower body regions, coronary sinus collects blood from wall of heart.

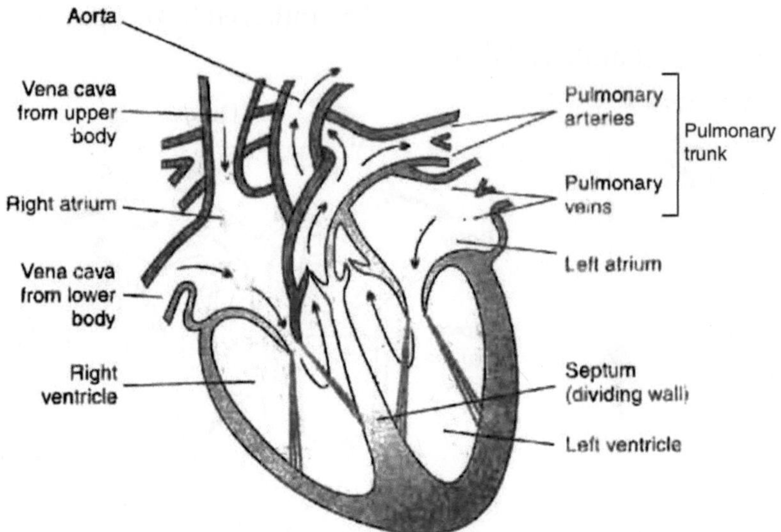

Fig. Internal structure of Human Heart

- Ventricles → left ventricle is longer & narrower than an right, left ventricle has thickest wall. Ventricles are separated by inter-ventricular septum.
- Pulmonary trunk arises from right ventricle & divides into right & left pulmonary arteries that carry deoxygenated blood to lungs. Opening of inferior vena cava is guarded by **eustachian valve**.
- At the base of pulmonary trunk & aorta semi-lunar valves are present.
- In right atrium adjoining to interatrial septum an oval depression, the fossa ovalis is present.
- At fossa ovalis the two atria are in communication with each other during foetal life but in adult it persists as depression. Bicuspid or mitral valve found between L.A and L.V.
- Tricuspid valve found between R.A and R.V.
- Attached to flaps of bicuspid & tricuspid valve are special **chordae tendineae** which are joined to other end of ventricular wall because of **papillary muscles**.
- Chordae tendineae prevent valves from collapsing back into atria during powerful ventricular contraction.

Working of Heart

- Heart is myogenic that means heart beat is initiated by a patch of heart muscle.
- **Path of conduction of Impulses :**

  S.A node (sinoatrial node / pacemaker) → situated in R.A near opening of superior vena cava.

  ↓

  A.V node (atrioventricular node or pacesetter) → situated in RA near or base of interartrial septum

  ↓

  Bundle of his → present in ventricles

  ↓

  Purkinje fibre → found in wall of heart

- **Cardiac cycle** → cardiac cycle consists of one heart beat. Time taken in one cycle is 0.8 sec.
  Out of which artrial systole is of 0.1 sec
  Ventricular systole is of 0.3 sec.
  Complete diastole is of 0.4 sec.

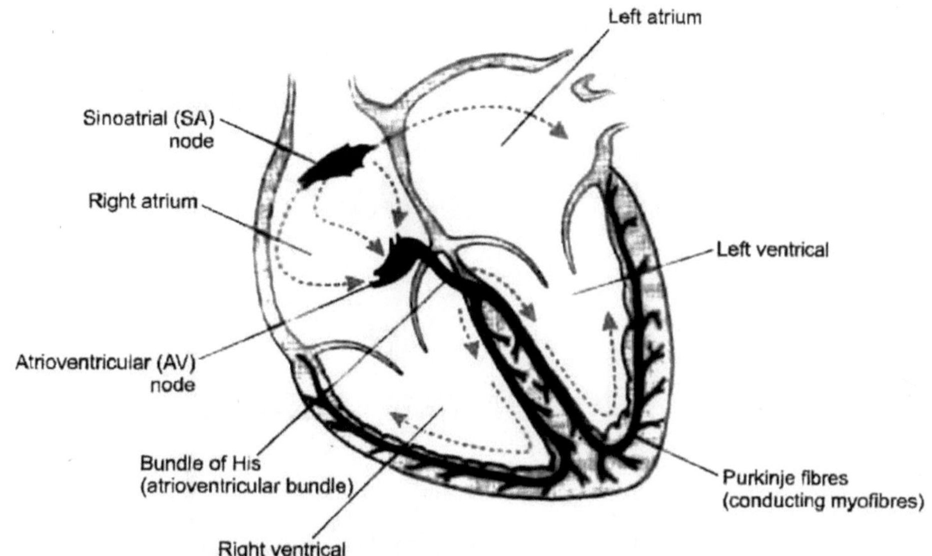

- **ECG -** A graphic record of the spread of the cardiac impulse through the heart is called **electrocardiogram**, process refer as **electrocardiography**.
- **Heart Beat :** Rhythmic expansion and contraction of heart is called **heart beat**. The relaxation is called diastole while the contraction is known as systole. The rate of heart beat is 70-72 / min in adult human males and 80/min in females. Heart beat is listened with the help of **stethoscope**.
- **Heart Sounds:**
  There is low pitched sound of longer duration called lubb and a high pitched sound of shorter duration known as **dupp**.

(i) The first sound "LUBB" is produced when the atrio-ventricular valves get closed sharply at the start of ventricular systole.

(ii) The second sound "DUPP" is produced when at the beginning of ventricular diastole, the semilunar valves at the roots of aorta and. pulmonary artery get closed.

Flow of Blood

- Vena cava brings de-oxygenated blood to right atrium.
- When right atrium is filled with blood it contract causing tricuspid valve to open. Blood is pushed into right ventricle.
- When right ventricle is filled, it contract and push blood into pulmonary artery (Tricuspid close, Pulmonary SLV open).
- Pulmonary artery carry blood to lungs for oxygenation (Pulmonary SLV prevents back flow).
- Oxygenated blood returns to heart by pulmonary vein.
- Pulmonary vein brings oxygenated blood to left auricle.
- Left auricle contract, blood passed to left ventricle (Bicuspid open).
- Left ventricle put blood into aorta, the largest artery (bicuspid close, aortic SLV open) which supplies to tissues.

Double circulation –

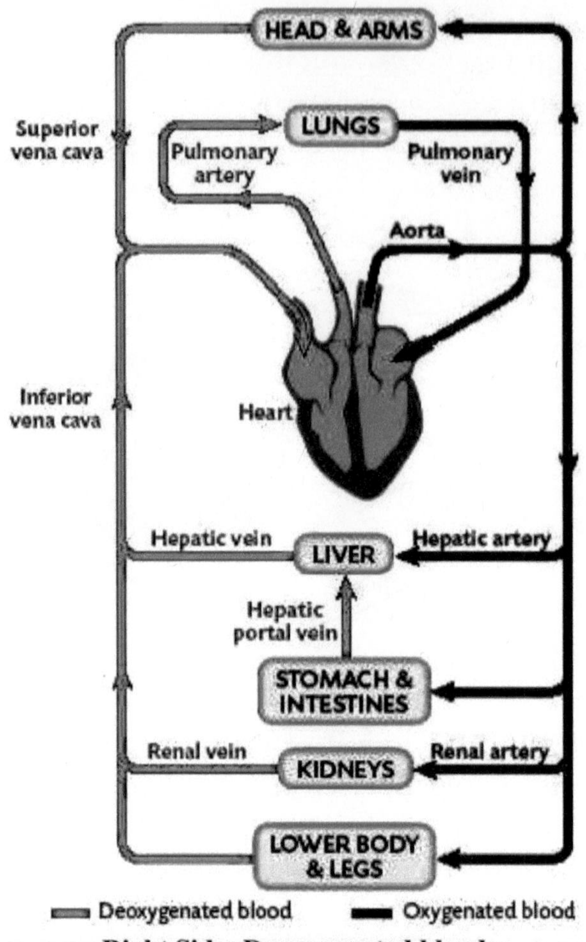

Right Side: Deoxygenated blood,
Left side: Oxygenated blood

- It was first discovered by **William Harvey (1578-1657).** Circulatory system of most terrestrial animals consists of two phase's. Blood passes from heart twice in one complete cycle, and it is called double circulation.
- It involves (a) Pulmonary circulation (b) Systemic circulation. Former is related to right side of heart and later related to left side of heart.
- Double Circulation prevents mixing of oxygenated blood present in left side and deoxygenated blood present in right side of heart.

Note : Fish have a single circulation system because they lack lungs and their heart has only two chambers with deoxygenated blood.

BLOOD PRESSURE

- Blood pressure (BP) is the pressure exerted by circulating blood upon the walls of arteries, and is one of the principal vital signs. Contraction of heart called **systole** and relaxation called **diastole**. During each heartbeat, BP varies between a maximum (systolic) when heart contracts (120 mm Hg) and a minimum (diastolic) pressure when heart expands (80 mm Hg). Blood Pressure is measured with help **SPHYGMOMANOMETER.**

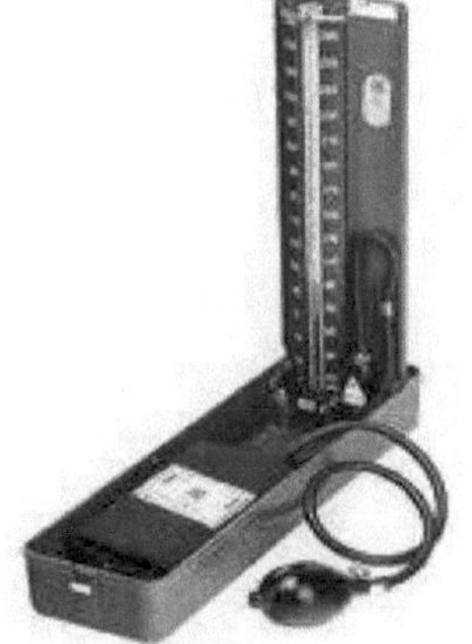

Figure: A Sphygmomanometer

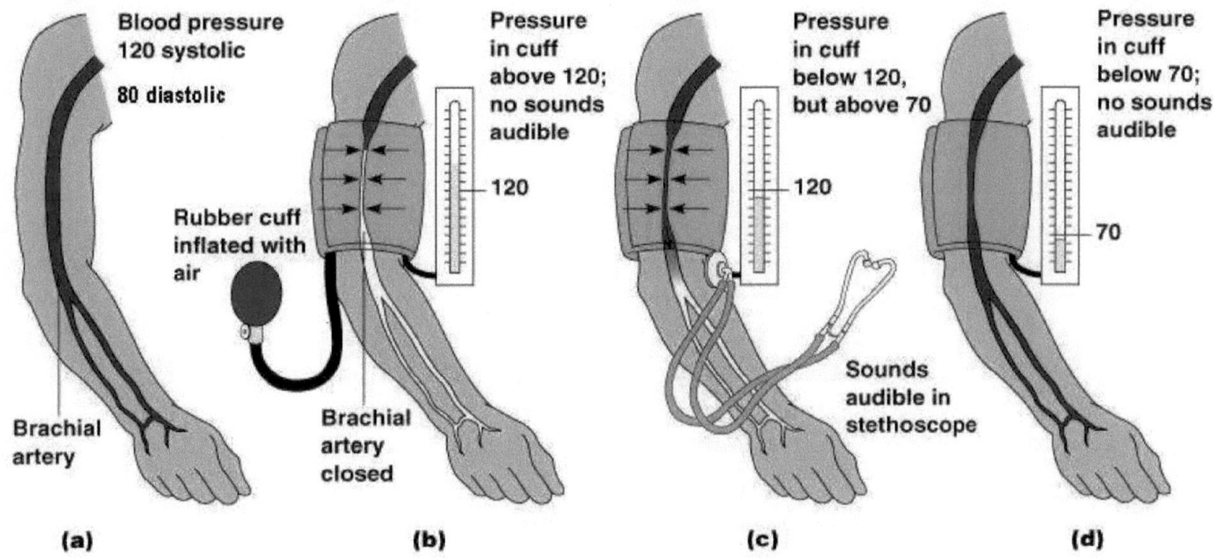

Figure : Steps of Measurement of Blood Pressure

- Constriction of arterioles, results in increased resistance to blood flow. This cause high blood pressure or hypertension. **Hypertension** can cause rupture of an artery and internal bleeding.
  Maintenance System : Platelets helps in plugging the injured site and preventing excess blood flow.
  Platelets or blood dust keeps on circulating in blood. At injury site, they come in contact with air and release a chemical known as **thromboplastin**, which triggers following changes:

$$\text{Injured Tissue} + \text{Blood platelets} \rightarrow \text{Release Thromboplastin}$$

$$\text{Prothrombin (Inactive)} \xrightarrow[+Ca^{++}]{\text{Thromboplastin}} \text{Thrombin (Active)}$$

$$\text{Fibrinogen (Soluble)} \xrightarrow[+Ca^{++}]{\text{Thrombin}} \text{Fibrin (Insoluble)}$$

$$\text{Fibrin} + \text{Red blood Corpuscles} \rightarrow \text{Blood clot}$$

LYMPH CIRCULATORY SYSTEM :

- It includes – lymph, lymph nodes and lymph vessels & capillaries

1. **Lymph** some amount of plasma, proteins and blood cells escape into intercellular space in the tissues to form the tissue fluid or lymph. Lymph (Blood - RBC) is an extra cellular, colourless fluid which moves in lymphatic system (Runs parallel to veins, towards heart).
   Functions of Lymph
   (a) Carry digested and absorbed fat from intestine back into blood.
   (b) It contains lymphocytes which help in killing germs.
2. **Lymph nodes** are kidney shaped structure. They are rich in lymphocytes.
3. **Lymph vessels and capillaries** – Tubular structure in which lymph flows, these vessels open into large veins of the body.

TRANSPORT IN PLANTS :

- Plants transport system helps in movement of food energy stored in leaves and raw materials from roots to various parts of plant.

- They perform conduction with help of vascular tissues (xylem and phloem).

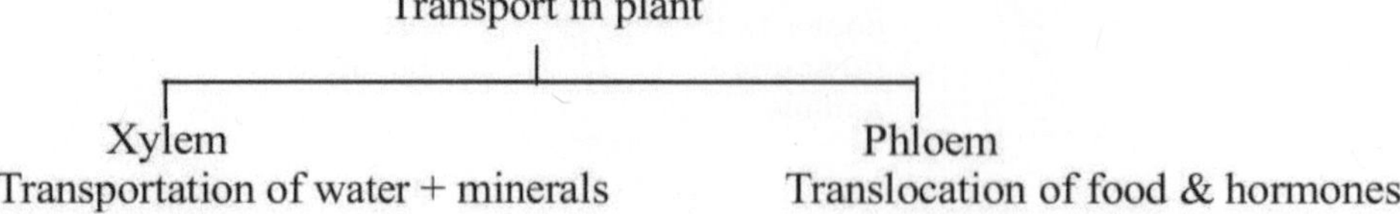

- Xylem is a complex permanent tissue that performs unidirectional transport and comprise of following components :

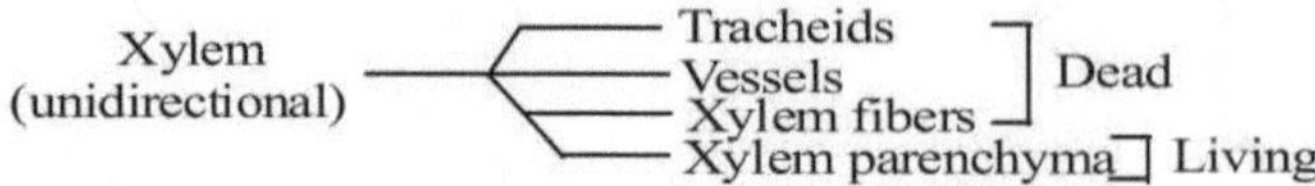

- **Ascent of Sap (upwards movement of water and mineral in Xylem from root to various parts of plant)**
- Vessels and tracheids in xylem of root, stem and leaves are interconnected to form a continuous system.
- Root absorbs water from soil through root hairs.
- There are various theories to explain movement of water from roots to upper parts of plant.
- **Most accepted theory of ascent of sap is cohesion tension theory**.
- **Dixon** and **Jolly** proposed that water is pulled up in plant by tension (negative pressure) from above. This suction pressure is created by **transpiration**
- Water is continually being lost from leaves by transpiration.
- Loss of water in the leaves exerts a pull on the water in the xylem ducts and draws more water into the leaf.
- A water molecule clings to each other by hydrogen bond **(cohesion)** which maintains strength in column.
- Because of the critical role of cohesion, the transpiration-pull theory is also called the cohesion theory.
- The rate of ascent of water is 10 – 75 **cm/min.**

Translocation of food :

- Food synthesized mainly in leaves and hormones synthesized at tip of root and shoots are transported by Phloem.
- Phloem uses energy for bidirectional transfer. It comprise of

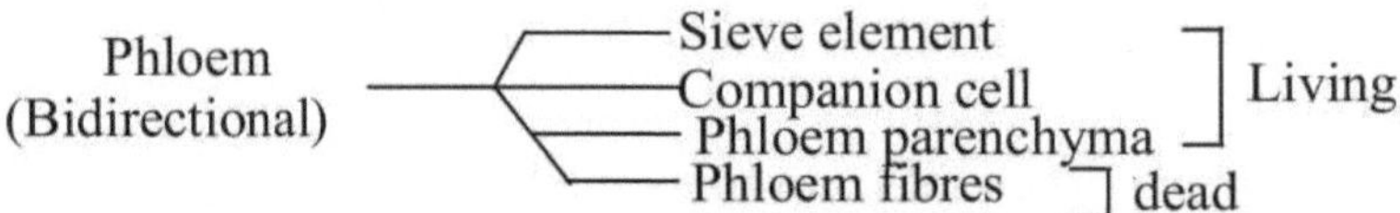

- Translocation of Food is best explained by **Munch hypothesis.**
- Food is produce in leaves **(source)** and used by other parts like root **(sink)**.
- Sucrose is transferred into **sieve tube** of phloem using ATP.
- This increase osmotic pressure of tissue causing water to move inside phloem.
- In the phloem, there is a continuous input of solute from source tissues (high pressure) and a continuous efflux at the sink (Low pressure).
- This input and output at the two ends will **maintain a pressure differential** that will keep liquid flowing.

- Thus, the driving force for solute transport is a **pressure gradient between the source and sink regions.** Speed of food transport is 60 – 100 **cm / hour.**

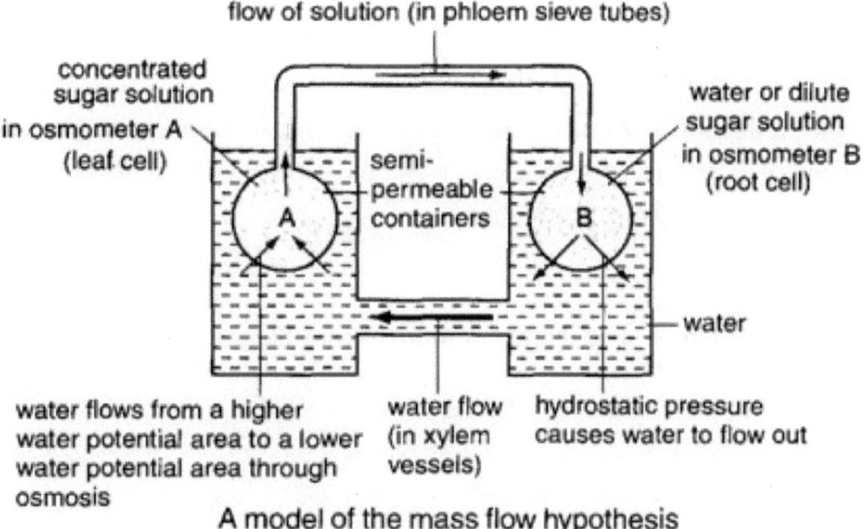

A model of the mass flow hypothesis

Difference in Xylem and Phloem

Xylem	Phloem
Mainly transport water and minerals	Mainly translocate food
Most part is dead.	Most part is living
Flow is unidirectional (Roots to Apex)	Flow is Bidirectional(Leaves to all parts)
No energy required (Physical force involved)	Energy is required
Located Superficially	Located Deeply

EXCRETION

Introduction :

- The different chemical activities in the body produce many by-products several of which are wastes.
- These waste products if allowed to accumulate will turn out to be toxic and affect the physiological activities of the body.
- These wastes have to be expelled out or it may eventually result in the death of the organism.

Definition :

- The removal of harmful and unwanted toxic waste products of metabolism is known as excretion.
- **Excretory System** is a system of organs and tissue that take part in separation, collection & Avoiding the waste produced.

Osmoregulation :

- The process by which the water content and the ion concentration is regulated and kept constant in the cells is known as osmoregulation.
- This process results in maintaining the osmotic pressure in the blood and tissue fluids.
- The two physiological processes, excretion and osmoregulation are interconnected as they both are responsible for bringing about homeostasis in the body.

- The physiological mechanisms involved are intimately bound with each other, so much so, in higher vertebrates like mammals, kidneys perform both functions, excretion and osmoregulation.
- The terms secretion and egestion are often confused with excretion. Hence it is important to understand clearly what they mean.

Secretion :

- Secretion is the production of useful chemical substances like hormones, enzymes or other molecules by the cells of glands like the bile, endocrine glands like the islets of Langerhans or unicellular glands like the epithelial mucosal lining of the large intestine.

Substances Excreted in Animals :

- The metabolic wastes which are excreted by animals may be grouped as follows:

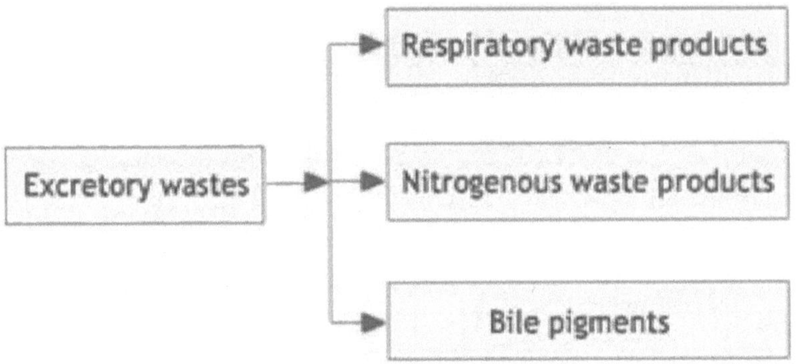

1. Respiratory Waste Products :

- Carbon dioxide and water are the by-products of catabolism of all varieties of foodstuffs.
- In lower animals carbon dioxide is eliminated directly into the environment through the body surface.
- In higher animals it is excreted out along with the exhaled air through the lungs.
- Excess water is excreted in the form of urine and sweat.

2. Nitrogenous Waste Products :

- Nitrogen containing waste products are derived from the deamination of the excess amino-acids consumed in the food and also from the breakdown of the proteins and nucleic acids.
- The following are the nitrogenous waste products produced by animals:

(i) Ammonia :

This is the main nitrogenous compound produced due to oxidative or deamination of amino acids during protein metabolism. Ammonia is highly toxic and it is important that it is expelled out of the body as and when it is formed as it can cause severe harm to the organism. i.e. **ammonotelism**. Eg. Fish, Amphibia.

(ii) Urea :

In higher animals ammonia combines with carbon dioxide in the liver and forms a less toxic substance called urea which is periodically flushed out of the system of the animal. Man eliminates nitrogenous waste in the form of urea. i.e. **ureotelism**. Eg. Human, animal (goat, dog and cow).

(iii) Uric Acid :

This is non-toxic and almost insoluble in water. Thus excretion of uric acid takes place with minimum loss of water. In man small quantities of uric acid is excreted in urine. In birds and reptiles, uric acid is excreted as a thick white paste or in the form of pellets. This enables these animals to conserve water. i.e. **uricotelism**. Eg. Reptiles and Aves.

(iv) Amino Acids :

Excess amino acids or proteins in higher animals are broken down into ammonia which are converted into less toxic substances like urea and uric acid in the liver. But in lower animals like molluscs and echinoderms the excess amino acid gets removed without undergoing any change

Excretion in Unicellular Organisms :

- Specific excretory organs are absent.
- Waste products (e.g., Ammonia, CO_2) generally pass out from the surface of the body into surrounding water by simple diffusion.
- Fresh water unicellular forms also posses an osmoregulatory organelle called **contractile vacuole**, e.g., Amoeba, Paramoecium.
- Contractile vacuole collects water and some wastes from the body, swells up (undergoes diastole), reaches the surface and bursts (undergoes systole) to release its contents to the outside.
- Osmoregulation is required in fresh water forms as fresh water has a tendency to enter their bodies due to higher internal osmotic concentration.

Excretion in Multicellular Organisms :

- Sponges and coelenterates do not have specific excretory organs as water bathes almost all their cells.
- Excretory structures appear for the first time in flatworms (platyhelminthes). They are flame cells.
- Nephridia are excretory organs of annelids, green glands in crustaceans, maphighian tubules in insects, and kidneys in molluscs.
- Kidneys form a urinary system in vertebrates.
- Some accessory excretory organs of vertebrates including human beings are skin, lungs and large intestine.

Table : Excretory Organs of different Animal groups

S.No.	Animal Groups	Excretory Organs
1	Protozoans (e.g. Amoeba, Paramoecium)	Plasma membrane
2.	Sponges (e.g. Sycon)	Plasma membrane of each cell.
3.	Cnidaria (e.g. Hydra)	Plasma membrane of each cell.
4.	Platyhelminthes (e.g. Planaria)	Flame cells (Solenocytes)
5.	Nemathelminthes (e.g. Ascaris)	H-shaped excretory system of canals and renette cells.
6.	Annelids (e.g. Neries, Earthworm)	Nephridia; chloragogen cells (yellow cells) in earthworm.
7.	Arthropods (a) Prawn (b) Most insects (c) Scorpion and Spiders	 Antennar / Green glands Malpighian tubules Malpighian tubules, coxal glands, hepatopancreas and nephrocytes.
8.	Molluscs (e.g. Unio, Pila)	Kidney. In Unio, kidney are called as **organ of Bojanus**.
9.	Echinoderms (e.g. Starfish)	Dermal branchiae and tube feet.
10.	Hemichordates (e.g. Balanoglossus)	Glomerulus.

Excretion and Osmoregulation in Man :

- Man is a highly evolved vertebrate and so the excretory organs are well developed.

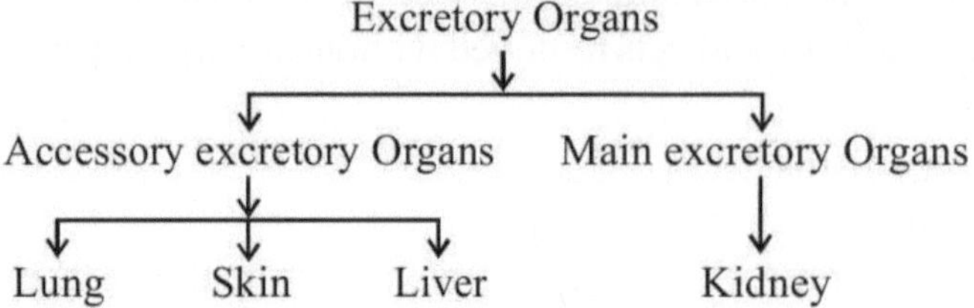

Main Excretory Organ Kidneys :

- The kidneys are the principal excretory organs in man through which the nitrogenous metabolic wastes are eliminated in the form of urine.

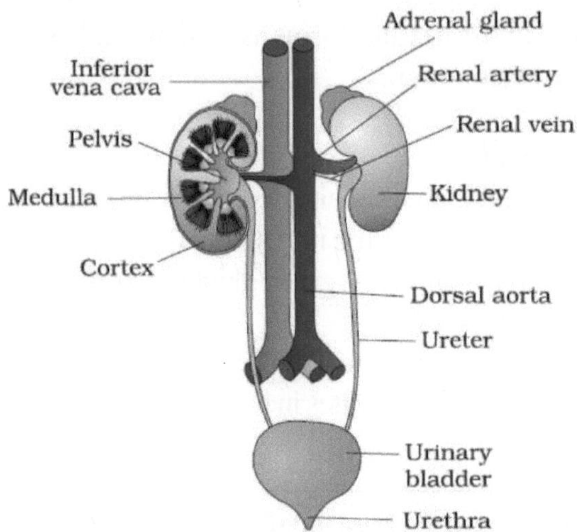

Human Excretory System

Do you know **:**

- The kidneys function as a pair of filters through which about one litre of blood circulates each minute.
- The entire blood in the body passes through them in 5 - 6 minutes. In a day it filters 1800 litres of blood which is 400 times the blood volume.
- Tea, coffee and alcohol are beverages that increase the formation of urine. They are termed diuretics.
- The human kidney contains more than 1.2 million nephrons.
- When a kidney is damaged or diseased, the other kidney is able to compensate for it. So a person can lead a normal life with only one kidney.
- A normal adult excretes 1 - 1.8 litres of urine per day.
- An artificial kidney (dialysing machine) is used for dialysis. When the kidneys of a patient stop functioning, life can be prolonged through dialysis.
- Kidney transplants have had good success rates and have given fresh lease of life to patients.

External Structure of kidneys :

- The kidneys are reddish brown, bean-shaped organs situated in the abdominal cavity, one on either side of the vertebral column in the lumbar region of the body.

- They lie asymmetrically, the right kidney being lower than the left as the right side of the abdominal cavity is occupied by the liver.
- Each kidney is 10 cm long, 6 cm wide and 4 cm thick and weighs 200 - 250 g in adults.
- A thin, tough, fibrous whitish capsule envelops each kidney.
- The outer surface of each kidney is convex while the inner surface is concave.
- Associated with the kidneys are the following:

1. Renal Artery :

The renal artery enters the kidney at the notch on the concave side called the hilus renalis. As it is a branch from the aorta it brings oxygenated blood carrying toxic nitrogenous wastes into the kidneys.

2. Renal Vein :

The renal vein drains away deoxygenated blood which is free of toxic substances into the inferior vena cava. This vein arises from the hilus of each kidney.

3. Ureter :

The ureter, a tube, runs from each kidney downwards into the lower part of the abdomen connecting each kidney to the urinary bladder. Its function is to transport the urine from the kidneys to the urinary bladder. The oblique entrance of the ureter into the bladder acts like a valve, preventing the back flow of urine from the bladder into the ureter.

4. Urinary Bladder :

This is a large muscular storage sac that collects urine from both the kidneys through the ureters. As the urine gets drained into the bladder its volume increases. The mouth of the bladder is guarded by a tight ring of muscle called the sphincter which regulates the opening or closing of the bladder. When the sphincter relaxes, urine is released out through the urethra.

5. Urethra :

This is a short muscular tube that carries urine at intervals from the urinary bladder to the outside. The base of the urethra is also guarded by a sphincter which keeps the urethra closed except while passing urine.

Internal Structure of kidney :

- A longitudinal section of the kidney shows three distinct regions:

1. Renal Cortex **2. Renal Medulla** **3. Renal Pelvis**

1. Renal Cortex :

This is the outer dark red layer. It contains the malphigian corpuscles, the proximal and distal parts of the renal tubule.

2. Renal Medulla :

This forms the inner pale zone and contains the Henle's loop and the collecting tubules, present in the form of renal pyramids. The conical pyramids project into the renal pelvis.

3. Renal Pelvis :

This is a large funnel-shaped region behind the renal medulla. Urine flows into the renal pelvis through minute openings at the tips or papillae of the pyramids. The urine that is collected is passed down to the ureters into the bladder.

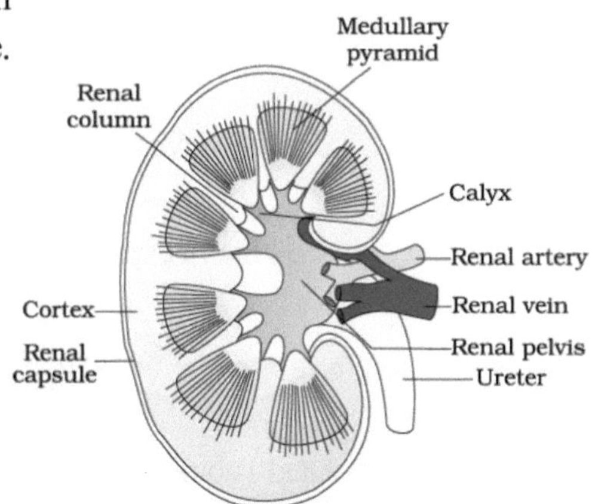

Longitudinal section (Diagrammatic) of Kidney

Each kidney consists of a large number of microscopic filtering units called nephrons. There are more than 1,250,000 nephrons in each kidney. Each nephron is about 30 - 40 mm. in length, originating in the cortex and extending into the medulla.

Microscopic Structure of a Nephron :

The nephron is the structural and functional unit of the kidney. Each nephron functions as an independent unit and produces a miniscule quantity of urine. The nephron can be differentiated into the following regions.

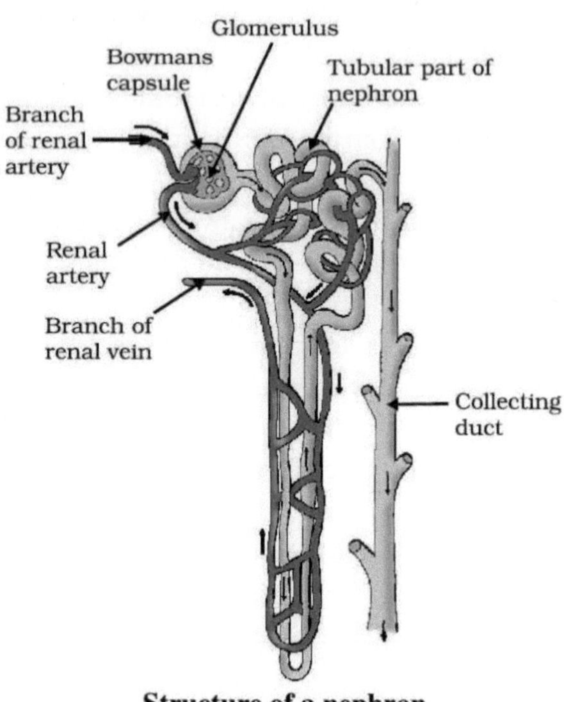

Structure of a nephron

Malpighian Corpuscle :

- This consists of two parts :

1. Bowman's Capsule :

This is a cup - shaped structure which is double walled in the hollow of which is a net work of capillaries called the **glomerulus**. (This is a knotted mass of blood capillaries formed by the afferent arteriole (incoming) and the efferent arteriole (outgoing)).

2. Renal Tubule :

This is the remaining part of the nephron, continuous with the Bowman's capsule. It is lined with ciliated epithelium and differentiated into the following regions :

(a) Proximal Convoluted Tubule (PCT) :

This is the region behind the Bowman's capsule and consists of a coiled tube that descends to form the Henle's loop. The proximal convoluted tubule is present in the cortex region.

(b) Henle's loop :

- This is continuous with the proximal convoluted tubule and is U-shaped having a narrow descending limb and a thick ascending limb. This part of the nephron descends from the cortex into the medulla region.

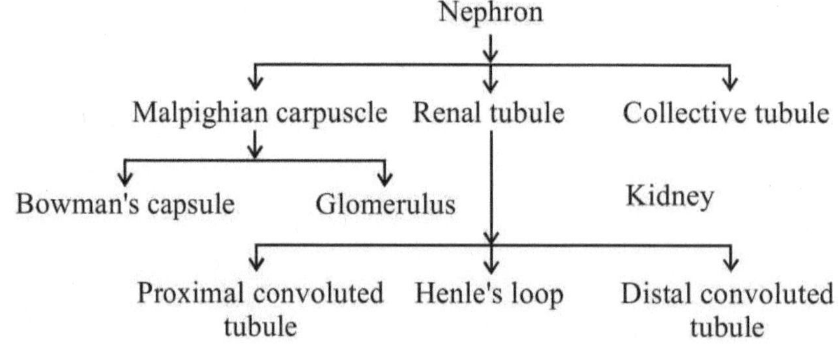

- Distal Convoluted Tubule (DCT)This is another coiled and twisted tubule that continues from the ascending limb of loop of Henle found in the renal cortex.

(c) Collecting Tubule :

- The distal convoluted tubule continues to form the collecting tubule.

(d) Collecting Ducts :

- Several collecting tubules fuse to form large collecting ducts which pass downwards from the cortex to the medulla region.

Do you know :

- Ducts of Bellini Several collecting ducts join to form the larger ducts of Bellini in the medulla region.
- Running through the pyramids they finally open in the renal pelvis draining all the urine collected from the various nephrons.
- The renal pelvis is an expanded region which opens into the ureter.
- **Vasa Rectae :** The efferent arteriole that exits from the glomerulus does not merge into a vein but breaks up into a system of capillaries called **vasa rectae** or **peritubular capillaries** which envelop the proximal convoluted tubule, the Henle's loop and distal convoluted tubule.
- These capillaries rejoin and drain into the venule.
- Venules join together to form the renal vein which drain blood from the kidneys.

Blood Flow In Kidney

Renal artery $\rightarrow$ Afferent arteriole $\rightarrow$ Glomerulus $\rightarrow$ Efferent arteriole $\rightarrow$ Venule $\rightarrow$ Renal vein

Micturition (Urination) :

- Urge for micturition occurs when urinary bladder comes to have 300-400 ml of urine.
- The stretched bladder stimulates nerve endings to develop the reflex.
- However, urine can be retained in the urinary bladder till it gets filled upto maximum capacity, 700 – 800 ml. At this time the urge becomes painful.
- Voluntary micturition can be carried any time.
- Total amount of urine excreted per day is about 1.6 – 1.8 litres.
- The quantity increases with larger intake of fluids and decreases with lesser intake of them.

URINE

- It is a transparent fluid produced by urinary system.
- Urine has an amber colour due to presence of urochrome.
- Urine contains 96% water, 2.5% organic substances and 1.5% inorganic solutes.
- Reaction is acidic in the beginning but becomes alkaline on standing due to decomposition of urea to form ammonia.

  Water - 96%

  Organic Substances – 2.5%, e.g., urea, uric acid, creatine, creatinise, water soluble vitamins, hormones, oxalate.

  Inorganic Solutes – 1.5%, e.g., sodium, chloride, phosphate, sulphate, magnesium, calcium, iodine.

Functions of Kidneys/Urinary or Excretory System :

(i) **Waste Products -** Excretion of nitrogenous and other waste products.

(ii) **Toxix Chemicals -** The system takes part in expelling toxic chemicals that happen to enter the body.

(iii) **Water Balance -** Maintenance of water balance in the bodyby producing dilute urine in excess when water intake is high and concentrated urine in case of lesser water intake or excessive sweating.

(iv) **Excess Materials -** Elimination of excess water soluble vitamins, drugs and other substances.

(v) **Regulation of Salt Content -** Regulation of salt content in body by excreting salts when in excess and retaining them when deficient.

(vi) **Maintenance of pH -** pH of body fluids is maintained by excretion or non-excretion of H^+ ion.

(vii) **Regulation of Blood Pressure -** By controlling the fluid content, kidneys regulate blood pressure.

ACCESSORY EXCRETORY ORGANS :

1. Skin - It contains sweat and sebaceous glands. Sweat glands excrete a fluid called sweat. Sweat consists of water (99.5%), traces of lactic acid, amino acids, urea and salt. Sebaceous glands secrete oil or sebum for lubricating hair. It has wax, sterols and other lipids.

2. Liver -

(i) Extra amino acids are deaminated and toxic ammonia is converted into less harmful urea in liver.

(ii) Liver degrades haemoglobin of worm out erythrocytes into bilirubin and biliverdin (bile pigments) for elimination.

(iii) It passes cholesterol, lecithin, excess vitamins, drugs and toxic substances into bile for elimination.

3. Lungs - They eliminate carbon dioxide and some aromatic substances.

4. Large Intestine - It excretes heavy metals and toxins into faecal matter.

RENAL FAILURE AND TECHNOLOGY FOR SURVIVAL

- The kidney slowly deteriorates and stops functioning.
- The symptoms are water retention, acidosis, anaemia and increase in blood urea level.
- You have learnt how important the kidneys are for survival.
- Though kidney failure is not common, sometimes kidney infection, injury to kidneys or restricted blood flow to kidneys result in kidney damage and malfunctioning.
- In order to clean the blood of metabolic wastes and to maintain normal levels of water and mineral ions in the body fluids, an 'artificial kidney' is employed as shown in the figure below.
- The procedure used in artificial kidney in place of the normal one is called dialysis.
- A matching kidney from another person may also be transplanted.

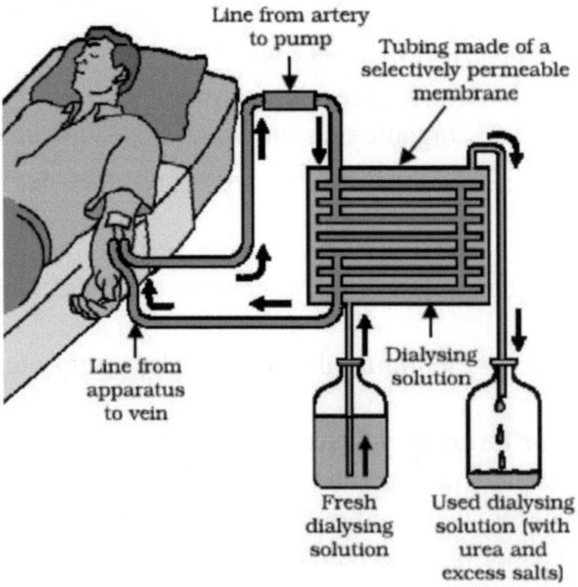

Artificial Kidney – Dialysis

Do You Know **:**

- Principle of dialysis Blood is made to flow into the dialysis machine made of long cellulose tubes coiled in a tank having a dialyzing solution.
- Waste substances diffuse out of blood into tank. The cleansed blood is pumped back into patient.

EXCRETION IN PLANTS :

- Plants do not produce nitrogenous wastes like urea and uric acid because extra amino acids and nucleotides are not formed.
- They produce other types of waste products, called secondary metabolites, e.g., alkaloids, tannins, aromatic oils.
- Excess of water is got rid off through transpiration. Excess of oxygen formed during day in photosynthesis organs can be considered as waste.
- It passes out through diffusion.
- The other wastes of plant metabolism are as follows :

(i) **Nitrogen Waste Products -** They are byproducts of general metabolism. The common ones are alkaloids, e.g., quinine, morphine, atropine.

(ii) **Organic Acids -** They are metabolic intermediates. Some of them are without any other use. Rather on accumulation they may prove toxic, e.g., oxalic acid.

(iii) **Tannins -** They are complex aromatic compounds which are formed as secondary metabolites.

(iv) **Latex -** It is an emulsion of varied composition which is exerted by special tubular cells called laticifers.

(v) **Resins -** They are oxidation products of aromatic oils.

(vi) **Gums -** They are degradation products of cell wall.

It saline habitates, the plants have to absorb excess salts that are required to be eliminated.

Mechanism :

Plants do not have any mechanism to collect, transport and throw out their waste products. They have adopted varied strategies to protect their living cells from waste products.

(i) **Old leaves -** Waste products are stored in older leaves which soon fall off.

(ii) **Old xylem -** Resins, gums, tannins and other waste products are deposited in the old xylem which soon becomes non-functional, e.g., heart wood.

(iii) **Bark -** Bark consits of dead cells which is peeled off periodically. Tannins and other wastes are deposited in the bark. Incidentally, tannins are raw maerial for dyes and inks.

(iv) **Central Vacuole -** Most plant waste products are stored in central vacuole of their cells. They are unable to influence the working of cytoplasm due to presence of a selectively permeable membrane called tonoplast.

(v) **Root Excretion -** Some waste substances are actually excreted by the plants in the region of their roots.

(vi) **Detoxification -** The toxic oxalic acid is detoxified by formation of calcium oxalate which gets crystallised into needle (raphides), prism (prismatic crystals), stars (sphaeraphides) and crystal sand. Excess of calcium is also precipitated as calcium carbonate crystals, e.g., cystolish.

(vii) **Salt Glands -** They excrete exces salts obtained from the habitat. Hydathodes also have an excretory function.

TRY YOURSELF :

1. Oxygen evolved during photosynthesis comes from
(A) CO_2 (B) H_2O (C) Both (A) and (B) (D) None of these

2. The atmosphere contains CO_2 by volume
(A) 0.1% (B) 0.5% (C) 0.03% (D) 0.3%

3. A cell that lacks chloroplast does not
(A) Evolve carbon dioxide (B) Liberate oxygen
(C) Require water (D) Utilize carbohydrates

4. Rate of photosynthesis is independent of
(A) Quality of light (B) NO_2 (C) Light duration (D) CO_2

5. Most effective wavelength of light for photosynthesis is
(A) Red (B) Yellow (C) Green (D) Violet

6. Photolysis of water takes place in
(A) Calvin cycle (B) Glycolysis (C) Light phase (D) Dark Phase

7. Man needs carbohydrates as a source of energy and he can get this energy from
(A) Cellulose (B) Starch (C) Both (A) and (B) (D) None of these

8. Trypsin converts
(A) Fats into fatty acids (B) Starch and glycogen into maltose
(C) Proteins into peptones (D) Sucrose into glucose and fructose

9. Liver cells secrete
(A) Lipase (B) Bile and no enzyme (C) Trypsin (D) Amylase

10. Glycogen is stored in
(A) Liver and muscles (B) Liver only (C) Pancreas (D) Muscles only

11. Gastric juice contains
(A) HCl (B) Renin (C) Pepsin (D) All of these

12. Saliva contains
(A) Ptyalin (B) Renin (C) Trypsin (D) All of these

13. Human digestive juices lack
(A) Lactase (B) Cellulase (C) Amylase (D) Lipase

14. In alimentary canal maximum absorption of water occurs in
(A) Rectum (B) Small intestine (C) Appendix (D) Stomach

15. The appendix in man is
(A) Vestigial (B) Involved in bile storage
(C) Similar to stomach in shape (D) Involved in digestion of vegetable

16. Which one of the following does not contribute to the breathing movements in mammals?
(A) Diaphragm (B) Larynx (C) Abdominal muscles (D) Ribs

17. A person with high fever may breath faster than normal. This may be due to
(A) Additional requirement of O_2 for the invaded germs
(B) High temperature of body
(C) Loss of appetite
(D) Mental worry of patient

18. A man respires about
(A) 40 times per minute (B) 72 times per minute
(C) 100 times per minute (D) 16–20 times per minutes

19. Tidal air in mammalian lungs is
(A) Total maximum air that can be drawn into lungs
(B) Air that normally goes in and comes out of lungs during breathing
(C) Air that is left in the lungs after normal expiration
(D) Air that can be expelled out from lungs forcibly after normal expiration.

20. The combination of haemoglobin with O_2 in the blood is inhibited by
(A) Decreasing O_2 concentration in blood (B) Increasing O_2 concentration in blood
(C) Increasing CO_2 concentration in blood (D) Introducing CO into blood

21. If a man from sea coast of Kerala goes to Mount everest.
(A) His breathing rate and heart beat will increase
(B) His breathing rate and heart beat will decrease
(C) His breathing rate will increase but heart beat will decrease
(D) His breathing rate will decrease but heart beat will increase

22. Heart is incompletely 4 chambered in
(A) Fishes (B) Amphibians (C) Reptiles (D) Birds

23. Valves are not found in
(A) Veins (B) Arteries (C) Heart (D) All of these

24. A person exercising hard shows the following except
(A) Decrease in blood glucose (B) Increase in lactic acid
(C) Increase in glycogen (D) None of these

25. Circulatory system is open in
(A) Prawn (B) Toad (C) Lizard (D) Pigeon

26. Normal blood pressure (systolic/diastolic) is_______mm of Hg
(A) 120/80 (B) 160/80 (C) 120/60 (D) 180/80

27. Heart beat initiates from
(A) Sino auricular node (B) Bundle of his
(C) Purkinje fibers (D) Auriculo ventricular node

28. Snake/animals living in desert are :
(A) Ureotelic (B) Uricotelic (C) Ammonotelic (D) Both (A) & (B)

29. Urinary bladder opens into :
(A) Uterus (B) Ureter (C) Urethra (D) None of these

30. Reabsorption of water in the kidney is under control of :
(A) ADH (B) ACTH (C) LH (D) PSH

31. A normal adult excrete_____ urine per day :
(A) 1–2 liters (B) 13–14 liters (C) 20–30liters (D) 12–15 liters

32. Structural and functional unit of kidney is :
(A) Glomerular (B) Loop of Henle (C) Malpighian body (D) Nephron

POINTS TO REMEMBER

1. Diaphragm becomes flat during inspiration and becomes convex during expiration.
2. **Tidal volume :** Volume of air inspired or expired in relaxed position. It is around 500 ml.
3. **Residual volume** : Air left in the whole respiratory tract after forceful expiration. It is 1.5 liters.
4. **Total lung capacity :** Maximum amount of air the lungs can hold after forceful inspiration. It is about 5-6.0 litres.
5. **Vital capacity :** Maximum amount of air which can be breathed out through forceful expiration after a forceful inspiration. It is 3.4-4.8 litres.
6. Vital Capacity is more in athletes, mountain dwellers, non smokers.
7. The total area for gas exchange provided by our 750 million alveoli in two lungs in 100 S. m.
8. In the cycle of inhalation and exhalation, repeated 15 to 18 times in a minutes about 500 ml of air is breathed in and out. In 24 hours, we breath in 1500 litres of air.
9. Blood is the medium for the transport of oxygen from the respiratory organ to the different tissues and carbon dioxide from tissues to the respiratory organs. As much as 97 percent of the oxygen is transported from the lungs to the tissues in combination with hemoglobin and only 2 percent is transported in dissolved condition by the plasma.
10. A normal person has about 15 grams of hemoglobin per 100 ml of blood. One gram of hemoglobin binds about 1.34 ml of O_2. Thus, 100 ml of blood carries about 20 ml of oxygen.
11. Carbon dioxide is also transported by hemoglobin. When a respiring tissue release carbon-dioxide, it is first diffused in the plasma. From here it diffuses into the red blood cells. Carbon-dioxide is transported from the tissues to the lungs in the form of bicarbonates dissolved in water.
12. About 23% of carbon dioxide entering into the erythrocytes combines with the globin (protein) part of haemoglobin to form carbaminohaemoglobin, which is transported to the lungs.
13. Carbon monoxide binds with hemoglobin about 230 times more readily than oxygen. When a person inhales carbon monoxide, it diffuses from the alveolar air to the blood and binds to haemoglobin forming carboxyhemoglobin. The latter is a relatively stable compound and cannot bind with oxygen molecules. So, the amount of hemoglobin available for oxygen transport is reduced. The resulting deficiency of oxygen cases headache, dizziness, nausea and even death.
14. **Mountain sickness :** It is also known as altitude sickness. At sea level the concentration of oxygen is about 21% and the barometric pressure averages 760 mm Hg. As altitude increases, the concentration remains the same but the number of oxygen molecules per breath is reduced. AT 12,000 feet the barometric pressure is only 483 mm Hg, so there are roughly 40% fewer oxygen molecules per breath. In order to oxygenate the body effectively, breathing rate (even while at rest) has to be increased. This extra ventilation increases the oxygen content in the blood, but not sea level concentration. The fall in oxygenation of blood produced the symptoms of mountain sickness. These symptoms include breathlessness, headache, dizziness, nausea, vomiting, mental fatigue and a bluish tinge on the skin, nails and lips.
15. The ability to perform the basic life processes distinguishes a living organism from a nonliving one.
16. Life processes are the vital processes carried out by living organisms in order to maintain and sustain life. Molecular movements are essential to carry out the various life processes.

17. Specialised body parts perform the various life processes in multicellular organisms. No such organs are present in unicellular organisms.

18. Energy required to carry out the different life processes, is obtained from carbon-based food sources through nutrition.

19. Depending on the mode of obtaining nutrition, organisms are classified as autotrophs or heterotrophs.

  a. Autotrophs can prepare their own food from simple inorganic sources like carbon dioxide and water. (eg- green plants, some bacteria)

  b. Heterotrophs cannot synthesize their own food and is dependent on the autotrophs for obtaining complex organic substances for nutrition. (eg. – animals)

20. Green plants prepare their food by the process of photosynthesis. Here, they utilize CO_2, H_2O and sunlight, with the help of chlorophyll, giving out O_2 as a byproduct.

21. In the light reaction of photosynthesis, light energy is absorbed and converted to chemical energy in the form of ATP. Also water molecules are split into hydrogen and oxygen.

22. Photosynthesis involves light-dependent reaction having non-cyclic and cyclic photophosphorylation and dark reaction where energy is utilised.

23. In 1941, by using Van Niel's hypothesis and the rare isotope of oxygen ^{18}O, water labelled with ^{18}O was used. The experiment proved that **all oxygen evolved comes from water only** and hence the modified equation of photosynthesis is written as given.

$$6CO_2 + 12\ H_2{}^{18}O \xrightarrow[\text{Chlorophyll}]{\text{Light energy}} C_6H_{12}O_6 + 6\,{}^{18}O_2 \quad + 6H_2O$$

24. In sulphur bacteria, he found that sulphur was released, not oxygen meaning that CO_2 was not split rather H_2S was broken down, and hydrogen reduced the CO_2.

$$6CO_2 + 12H_2S \xrightarrow[\text{Chlorophyll}]{\text{Light energy}} C_6H_{12}O_6 + 12S \quad + H_2O$$

25. By 1950 it was well established that both the reactions occur in separate areas, the light reaction takes place on the chloroplast membranes and the dark reaction in the stroma region.

26. Desert plants as an exception, opens stomata in night to absorb CO_2 and form intermediate compound i.e. malate which is stored in vacuole. During day it is converted into sugar.

27. The parasite, the one that draws nourishment often lacks digestive system as it feeds on nutrients already in solution form or digested form, from the host as in the case of gut parasites like tapeworm and round worm.

28. Commercially for curdling of milk the **Rennet tablets** are used which contain renin extracted from the calf gastric mucosa.

29. Carbon dioxide is reduced to carbohydrates in the dark phase of photosynthesis.

30. Plants carry out gaseous exchange with surrounding through stomata.

31. Heterotrophs may be herbivores, carnivores, parasites or saprophytes.

32. In Amoeba, digestion occurs in the food vacuole, formed by the engulfing of food by its pseudopodia.

33. In humans, digestion of food takes place in the alimentary canal, made up of various organs and glands.

34. In mouth, food is crushed into small particles through chewing and mixed with saliva, which contains amylase for digesting starch.

35. On swallowing, food passes through pharynx and oesophagus to reach stomach. The gastric juice contains pepsin (for digesting proteins), HCl and mucus.
36. Liver secretes bile which emulsifies fat.
37. Pancreatic juice contains enzymes amylase, trypsin and lipase for digesting starch, proteins and fats respectively.
38. In the small intestine, carbohydrate, proteins and fats are completely digested into glucose, amino acids, and fatty acids and glycerol respectively.
39. The villi of small intestine absorb the digested food and supply it to every cell of the body.
40. The undigested food is egested from the body through anus.
41. During respiration, the digested food materials are broken down to release energy in the form of ATP.
42. Depending on the requirement of oxygen, respiration may be

    a. Aerobic - occurring in presence of oxygen or

    b. Anaerobic – occurring in absence of oxygen.
43. The end-products are lactic acid or ethanol + CO_2, in anaerobic respiration or CO_2 and water in aerobic respiration. Large amount of energy is released in aerobic respiration as compared to anaerobic respiration.
44. Plants release CO_2 at night and oxygen during the day.
45. Terrestrial organisms use atmospheric oxygen for respiration whereas aquatic organisms use the dissolved oxygen in water.
46. In humans, air takes the following path on entering the nostrils.

    Nostrils $\rightarrow$ Nasal passage $\rightarrow$ Pharynx $\rightarrow$ Larynx $\rightarrow$ Trachea $\rightarrow$ Bronchus $\rightarrow$ Bronchiole $\rightarrow$ Alveolus.
47. The alveoli of lungs are richly supplied with blood and are the sites where exchange of gases (O_2 and CO_2) occurs between blood and atmosphere.
48. In humans, the respiratory pigment haemoglobin, carry oxygen from lungs to different tissues of the body.
49. Acetyl Co-A is a important molecule in metabolism. It main function is to convey the carbon atom with in acetyl group to the citric acid cycle to be oxidized to produced energy.
50. In humans, the circulatory system transports various materials throughout the body and is composed of the heart, blood and blood vessels.
51. Human heart has 4 chambers – 2 atria (right and left) and 2 ventricles (right and left). Right half of the heart receives deoxygenated blood whereas the left half receives oxygenated blood.
52. Cockroach has 13 hearts.
53. Ventricular walls are much thicker than atrial walls.
54. Arteries carry blood from heart to different parts of the body whereas veins deliver the blood back to the heart. Arteries are connected to veins by thin capillaries, wherein materials are exchanged between blood and cells.
55. Humans show double circulation and complete separation of oxygenated and deoxygenated blood.
56. Blood platelets are essential for clotting of blood at the place of injury and thus preventing blood loss.
57. Lymphatic system consists of lymph, lymph nodes, lymphatic capillaries and lymph vessels which drain into larger veins. Lymph is also important in the process of transportation.

58. In plants, water is transported through the xylem tissue, from roots to the aerial parts of the plant. Root pressure and transpiration pull are the major forces involved in pulling water up the xylem.

59. Translocation of food is carried out through phloem tissue from leaves and storage organs to other parts of the plant. This process requires energy from ATP.

60. During excretion, the harmful metabolic nitrogenous wastes generated are removed from the body.

61. In humans, a pair of kidneys, a pair of ureters, urinary bladder and urethra constitutes the excretory system.

62. Nephrons are the basic filtration units of kidneys. They carry out filtration, selective reabsorption and tubular secretion to form urine in kidney, which is then passed out through the urethra, via the ureters and urinary bladder.

63. Plants do not have an excretory system and carries out excretion in various ways like transpiration, releasing wastes into surrounding soil, losing the leaves and storing in cell vacuoles and in old xylem.

64. **Ornithine cycle** – Ornithine cycle is the process of converting ammonia into urea by combining with CO_2 in liver.

CONCEPT APPLICATION LEVEL - I [NCERT Questions]

Q.1 Why is diffusion insufficient to meet the oxygen requirements of multi-cellular organisms like humans?

Ans. Multicellular organisms such as humans possess complex body designs. They have specialised cells and tissues for performing various necessary functions of the body such as intake of food and oxygen. Unlike unicellular organisms, multicellular cells are not in direct contact with the outside environment. Therefore, diffusion cannot meet their oxygen requirements.

Q.2 What criteria do we use to decide whether something is alive?

Ans. Any visible movement such as walking, breathing, or growing is generally used to decide whether something is alive or not. However, a living organism can also have movements, which are not visible to the naked eye. Therefore, the presence of life processes is a fundamental criterion that can be used to decide whether something is alive or not.

Q.3 What are outside raw materials used for by an organism?

Ans. An organism uses outside raw materials mostly in the form of food and oxygen. The raw materials required by an organism can be quite varied depending on the complexity of the organism and its environment.

Q.4 What processes would you consider essential for maintaining life?

Ans. Life processes such as nutrition, respiration, transportation, excretion, etc. are essential for maintaining life.

Q.5 What are the differences between autotrophic nutrition and heterotrophic nutrition?

Ans.

	Autotrophic nutrition	Heterotrophic nutrition
(i)	Food is synthesised from simple inorganic raw materials such as CO_2 and water.	Food is obtained directly or indirectly from autotrophs. This food is broken down with the help of enzymes.
(ii)	Presence of green pigment (chlorophyll) is necessary.	No pigment is required in this type of nutrition.
(iii)	Food is generally prepared during day time.	Food can be prepared at all times.
(iv)	All green plants and some bacteria have this type of nutrition.	All animals and fungi have this type of nutrition.

Q.6 Where do plants get each of the raw materials required for photosynthesis?

Ans. The following raw materials are required for photosynthesis :

- The raw material CO_2 enters from the atmosphere through stomata.
- Water is absorbed from the soil by the plant roots.
- Sunlight, an important component to manufacture food, is absorbed by the chlorophyll and other green parts of the plants.

Q.7 What is the role of the acid in our stomach?

Ans. The hydrochloric acid present in our stomach dissolves bits of food and creates an acidic medium. In this acidic medium, enzyme pepsinogen is converted to pepsin, which is a protein-digesting enzyme.

Q.8 What is the function of digestive enzymes?

Ans. Digestive enzymes such as amylase, lipase, pepsin, trypsin, etc. help in the breaking down of complex food particles into simple ones. These simple particles can be easily absorbed by the blood and thus transported to all the cells of the body.

Q.9 How is the small intestine designed to absorb digested food?

Ans. The small intestine has millions of tiny finger-like projections called villi. These villi increase the surface area for more efficient food absorption. Within these villi, many blood vessels are present that absorb the digested food and carry it to the blood stream. From the blood stream, the absorbed food is delivered to each and every cell of the body.

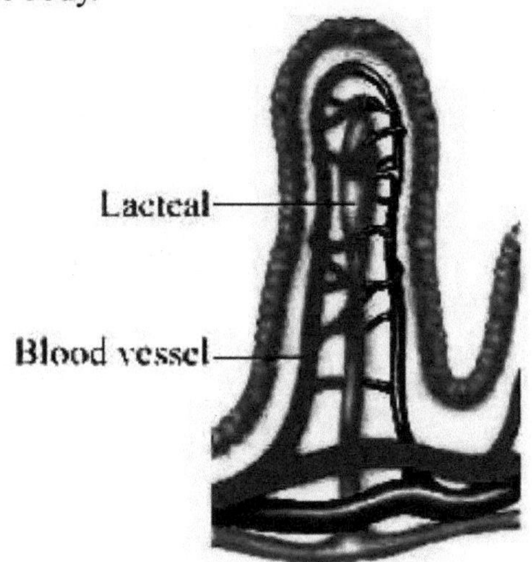

Enlarged view of a villus

Q.10 What advantage over an aquatic organism does a terrestrial organism have with regard to obtaining oxygen for respiration?

Ans. Terrestrial organisms take up oxygen from the atmosphere whereas aquatic animals need to utilize oxygen present in the water. Air contains more O_2 as compared to water. Since the content of O_2 in air is high, the terrestrial animals do not have to breathe faster to get more oxygen. Therefore, unlike aquatic animals, terrestrial animals do not have to show various adaptations for better gaseous exchange.

Q.11 What are the different ways in which glucose is oxidized to provide energy in various organisms?

Ans. Glucose is first broken down in the cell cytoplasm into a three carbon molecule called pyruvate. Pyruvate is further broken down by different ways to provide energy.

The breakdown of glucose by different pathways can be illustrated as follows.

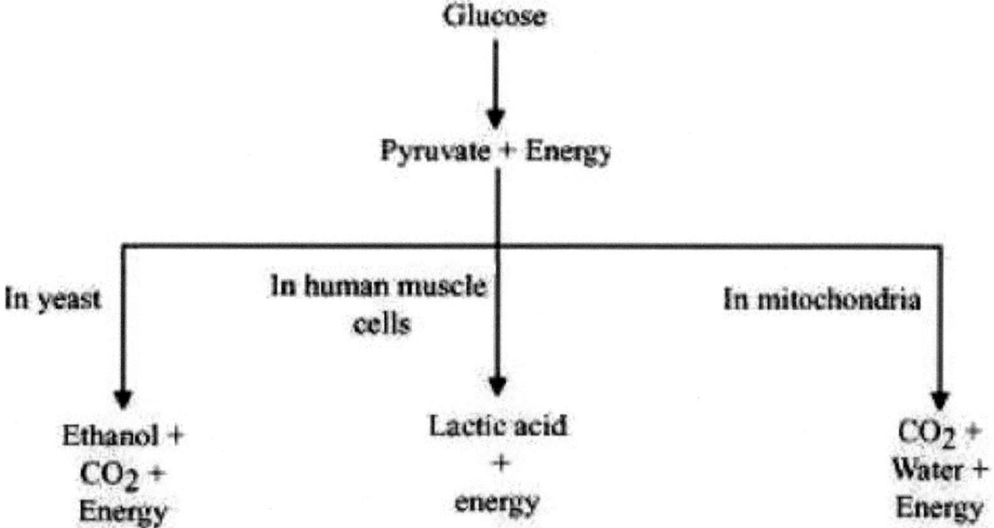

In yeast and human muscle cells, the breakdown of pyruvate occurs in the absence of oxygen whereas in mitochondria, the breakdown of pyruvate occurs in the presence of oxygen.

Q.12 How is oxygen and carbon dioxide transported in human beings?

Ans. Haemoglobin transports oxygen molecule to all the body cells for cellular respiration. The haemoglobin pigment present in the blood gets attached to four O_2 molecules that are obtained from breathing. It thus forms oxyhaemoglobin and the blood becomes oxygenated. This oxygenated blood is then distributed to all the body cells by the heart. After giving away O_2 to the body cells, blood takes away CO_2 which is the end product of cellular respiration. Now the blood becomes de-oxygenated.
Since haemoglobin pigment has less affinity for CO_2, CO_2 is mainly transported in the dissolved form. This de-oxygenated blood gives CO_2 to lung alveoli and takes O_2 in return.

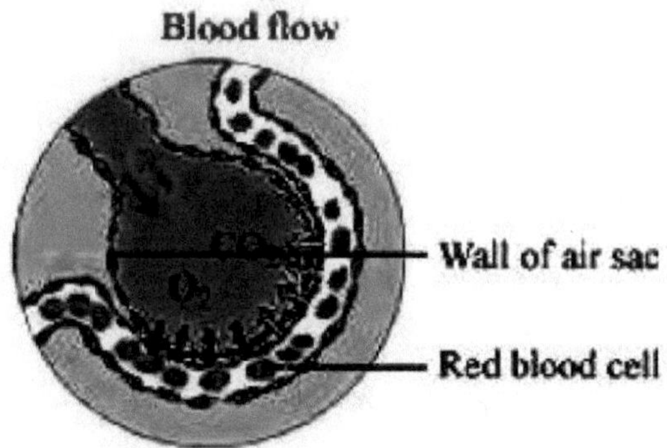

Transportation of O_2 and CO_2 in blood.

Q.13 How are the lungs designed in human beings to maximize the area for exchange of gases?

Ans. The exchange of gases takes place between the blood of the capillaries that surround the alveoli and the gases present in the alveoli. Thus, alveoli are the site for exchange of gases. The lungs get filled up with air during the process of inhalation as ribs are lifted up and diaphragm is flattened. The air that is rushed inside the lungs fills the numerous alveoli present in the lungs. Each lung contains 300-350 million alveoli. These numerous alveoli increase the surface area for gaseous exchange making the process of respiration more efficient.

Q.14 What are the components of the transport system in human beings? What are the functions of these components?

Ans. The main components of the transport system in human beings are the heart, blood, and blood vessels.

- Heart pumps oxygenated blood throughout the body. It receives deoxygenated blood from the various body parts and sends this impure blood to the lungs for oxygenation.
- Being a fluid connective tissue, blood helps in the transport of oxygen, nutrients, CO_2, and nitrogenous wastes.
- The blood vessels (arteries, veins, and capillaries) carry blood either away from the heart to various organs or from various organs back to the heart.

Q.15 Why is it necessary to separate oxygenated and deoxygenated blood in mammals and birds?

Ans. Warm-blooded animals such as birds and mammals maintain a constant body temperature by cooling themselves when they are in a hotter environment and by warming their bodies when they are in a cooler environment. Hence, these animals require more oxygen (O_2) for more cellular respiration so that they can produce more energy to maintain their body temperature.

Thus, it is necessary for them to separate oxygenated and de-oxygenated blood, so that their circulatory system is more efficient and can maintain their constant body temperature.

Q.16 What are the components of the transport system in highly organised plants?

Ans. In highly organised plants, there are two different types of conducting tissues - xylem and phloem. Xylem conducts water and minerals obtained from the soil (via roots) to the rest of the plant. Phloem transports food materials from the leaves to different parts of the plant body.

Q.17 How are water and minerals transported in plants?

Ans. The components of xylem tissue (tracheids and vessels) of roots, stems, and leaves are interconnected to form a continuous system of water-conducting channels that reaches all parts of the plant. Transpiration creates a suction pressure, as a result of which water is forced into the xylem cells of the roots. Then there is a steady movement of water from the root xylem to all the plant parts through the interconnected water-conducting channels.

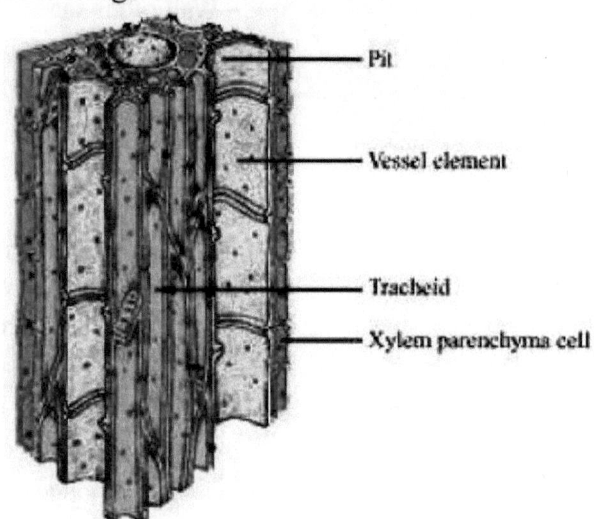

Components of xylem tissue

Q.18 How is food transported in plants?

Ans. Phloem transports food materials from the leaves to different parts of the plant body. The transportation of food in phloem is achieved by utilizing energy from ATP. As a result of this, the osmotic pressure in the tissue increases causing water to move into it. This pressure moves the material in the phloem to the tissues which have less pressure. This is helpful in moving materials according to the needs of the plant. For example, the food material, such as sucrose, is transported into the phloem tissue using ATP energy.

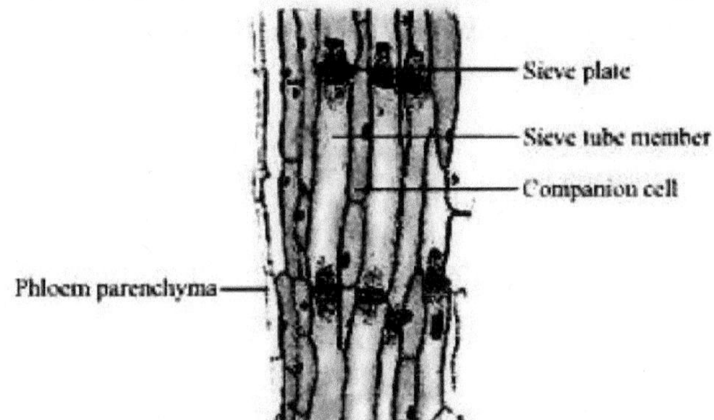

Components of phloem tissue

Q.19 Describe the structure and functioning of nephrons.

Ans. Nephrons are the basic filtering units of kidneys. Each kidney possesses large number of nephrons, approximately 1-1.5 million. The main components of the nephron are glomerulus, Bowman's capsule, and a long renal tubule.

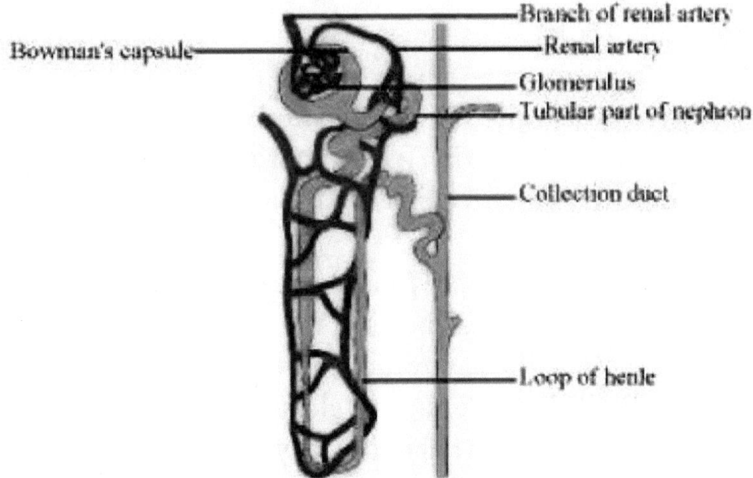

Structure of a nephron

Functioning of a nephron :

- The blood enters the kidney through the renal artery, which branches into many capillaries associated with glomerulus.
- The water and solute are transferred to the nephron at Bowman's capsule.
- In the proximal tubule, some substances such as amino acids, glucose, and salts are selectively reabsorbed and unwanted molecules are added in the urine.
- The filtrate then moves down into the loop of Henle, where more water is absorbed.
- From here, the filtrate moves upwards into the distal tubule and finally to the collecting duct. Collecting duct collects urine from many nephrons.
- The urine formed in each kidney enters a long tube called ureter. From ureter, it gets transported to the urinary bladder and then into the urethra.

Q.20 What are the methods used by plants to get rid of excretory products?

Ans. Plants can get rid of excess of water by transpiration. Waste materials may be stored in the cell vacuoles or as gum and resin, especially in old xylem. It is also stored in the leaves that later fall off.

Q.21 How is the amount of urine produced regulated?

Ans. The amount of urine produced depends on the amount of excess water and dissolved wastes present in the body. Some other factors such as habitat of an organism and hormone such as Antidiuretic hormone (ADH) also regulates the amount of urine produced.

Q.22 The kidneys in human beings are a part of the system for
(a) nutrition. (b) respiration. (c) excretion. (d) transportation.

Ans. **(c)** In human beings, the kidneys are a part of the system for excretion.

Q.23 The xylem in plants are responsible for
(a) transport of water. (b) transport of food.
(c) transport of amino acids. (d) transport of oxygen.

Ans. **(a)** In a plant, the xylem is responsible for transport of water.

Q.24 The autotrophic mode of nutrition requires
(a) carbon dioxide and water. (b) chlorophyll.
(c) sunlight. (d) all of the above.

Ans. **(d)** The autotrophic mode of nutrition requires carbon dioxide, water, chlorophyll and sunlight.

Q.25 The breakdown of pyruvate to give carbon dioxide, water and energy takes place in
(a) cytoplasm. (b) mitochondria. (c) chloroplast. (d) nucleus.

Ans. **(b)** The breakdown of pyruvate to give carbon dioxide, water and energy takes place in mitochondria.

Q.26 How are fats digested in our bodies? Where does this process take place?

Ans. Fats are present in the form of large globules in the small intestine. The small intestine gets the secretions in the form of bile juice and pancreatic juice respectively from the liver and the pancreas. The bile salts (from the liver) break down the large fat globules into smaller globules so that the pancreatic enzymes can easily act on them. This is referred to as emulsification of fats. It takes place in the small intestine.

Q.27 What is the role of saliva in the digestion of food?

Ans. Saliva is secreted by the salivary glands, located under the tongue. It moistens the food for easy swallowing. It contains a digestive enzyme called salivary amylase, which breaks down starch into sugar.

Q.28 What are the necessary conditions for autotrophic nutrition and what are its by-products?

Ans. Autotrophic nutrition takes place through the process of photosynthesis. Carbon dioxide, water, chlorophyll pigment, and sunlight are the necessary conditions required for autotrophic nutrition. Carbohydrates (food) and O_2 are the by-products of photosynthesis.

Q.29 What are the differences between aerobic and anaerobic respiration? Name some organisms that use the anaerobic mode of respiration.

Ans.

Aerobic Respiration	Anaerobic Respiration
1. **Method.** It is the common method of respiration.	It occurs permanently only in a few organism. In others it may occur as a temporary measure to overcome shortage of oxygen.
2. **Steps.** It is completed in 3 steps – glycolysis, Krebs cycle and terminal oxidation.	There are two steps – glycolysis and anaerobic breakdown of pyruvic acid.
3. **Oxygen.** It requires oxygen.	Oxygen is not required.
4. **Breakdown.** Respiratory substrate is completely broken down.	Respiratory substrate is incompletely broken down.
5. **End Products.** They are inorganic.	Atleast one end product is organic. Inorganic products may or may not be present.
6. **Toxicity.** End products show little toxicity.	The organic end product is generally toxic.
7. **Occurance.** It occurs partly in cytoplasm and partly in mitochondria.	Anaerobic respiration is carried out entirely in cytoplasm. Mitochondria are not required.
8. **E.T.C.** An electron transport chain is required.	ETC is not required.
9. **Energy.** In release 686 kcal or 2870 kJ of energy per mole of glucose.	Energy liberated is 36-50 kcal or 150-210 kJ per mole of glucose.
10. ATP. The liberated energy issued in forming 36-38 ATP molecule per mole of glucose.	The liberate energy is used in synthesis of 2ATP mole.

Anaerobic respiration occurs in the roots of some waterlogged plants, some parasitic worms, animal muscles, and some micro-organisms such as yeasts.

Q.30 How are the alveoli designed to maximise the exchange of gases?

Ans. The alveoli are the small balloon-like structures present in the lungs. The walls of the alveoli consist of extensive network of blood vessels. Each lung contains 300-350 million alveoli, making it a total of approximately 700 million in both the lungs. The alveolar surface when spread out covers about 80 m^2 area. This large surface area makes the gaseous exchange more efficient.

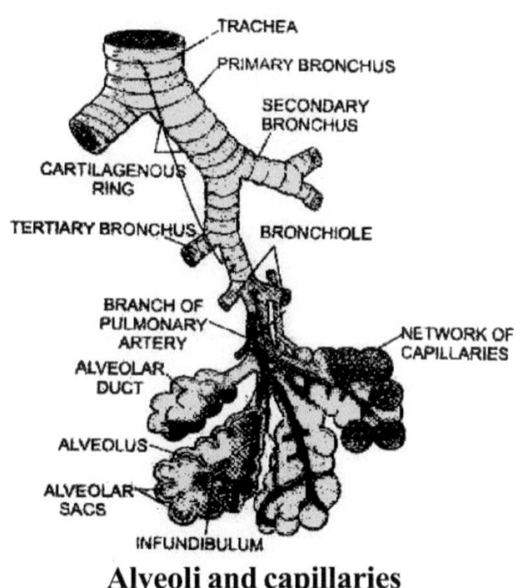

Alveoli and capillaries

Q.31 What would be the consequences of a deficiency of haemoglobin in our bodies?

Ans. Haemoglobin is the respiratory pigment that transports oxygen to the body cells for cellular respiration. Therefore, deficiency of haemoglobin in blood can affect the oxygen supplying capacity of blood. This can lead to deficiency of oxygen in the body cells. It can also lead to a disease called anaemia.

Q.32 Describe double circulation in human beings. Why is it necessary?

Ans. The human heart is divided into four chambers - the right atrium, the right ventricle, the left atrium, and the left ventricle.

Flow of blood in the heart

- The heart has superior and inferior vena cava, which carries de-oxygenated blood from the upper and lower regions of the body respectively and supplies this de-oxygenated blood to the right atrium of the heart.

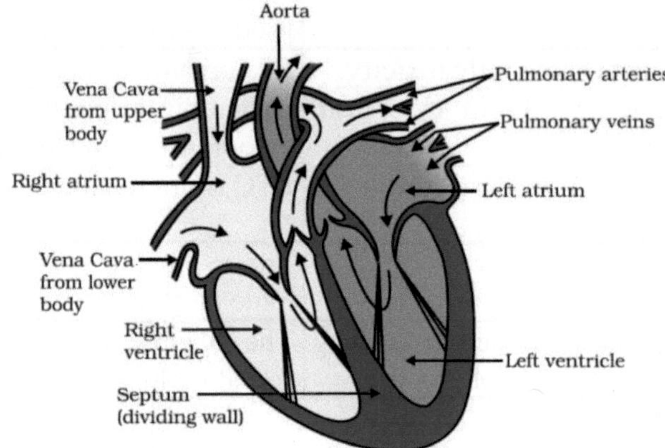

Flow of blood in the heart

- The right atrium then contracts and passes the de-oxygenated blood to the right ventricle, through an auriculo-ventricular aperture.
- Then the right ventricle contracts and passes the de-oxygenated blood into the two pulmonary arteries, which pumps it to the lungs where the blood becomes oxygenated. From the lungs, the pulmonary veins transport the oxygenated blood to the left atrium of the heart.
- Then the left atrium contracts and through the auriculo-ventricular aperture, the oxygenated blood enters the left ventricle.
- The blood passes to aorta from the left ventricle. The aorta gives rise to many arteries that distribute the oxygenated blood to all the regions of the body.

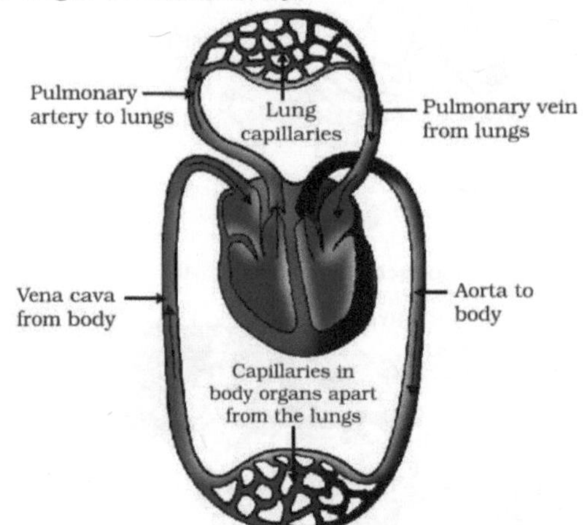

Schematic diagram of blood circulation in humans

- Therefore, the blood goes twice through the heart. This is known as double circulation.

Importance of double circulation :

- The separation of oxygenated and de-oxygenated blood allows a more efficient supply of oxygen to the body cells. This efficient system of oxygen supply is very useful in warm-blooded animals such as human beings.
- As we know, warm-blooded animals have to maintain a constant body temperature by cooling themselves when they are in a hotter environment and by warming their bodies when they are in a cooler environment. Hence, they require more O2 for more respiration so that they can produce more energy to maintain their body temperature. Thus, the circulatory system of humans is more efficient because of the double circulatory heart.

Q.33 What are the differences between the transport of materials in xylem and phloem?

Ans.

	Transport of materials in xylem	**Transport of materials in phloem**
(i)	Xylem tissue helps in the transport of water and minerals.	Phloem tissue helps in the transport of food.
(ii)	Water is transported upwards from roots to all	Food is transported in both upward and downward directions.
(iii)	Transport in xylem occurs with the help of simple physical forces such as transpiration pull.	Transport of food in phloem requires energy in the form of ATP.

Q.34 Compare the functioning of alveoli in the lungs and nephrons in the kidneys with respect to their structure and functioning.

Ans.

Alveoli	Nephron
Structure (i) Alveoli are tiny balloon-like structures present inside the lungs. (ii) The walls of the alveoli are one cell thick and it contains an extensive network of blood capillaries. 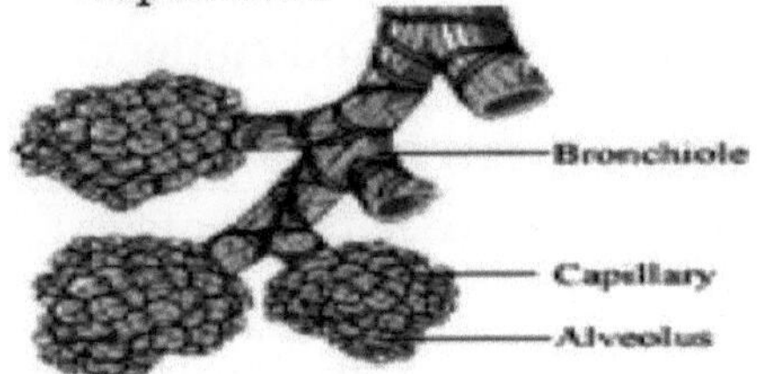	**Structure** (i) Nephrons are tubular structures present inside the kidneys. (ii) Nephrons are made of glomerulus, bowman's capsule, and a long renal tube. It also contains a cluster of thin walled capillaries. 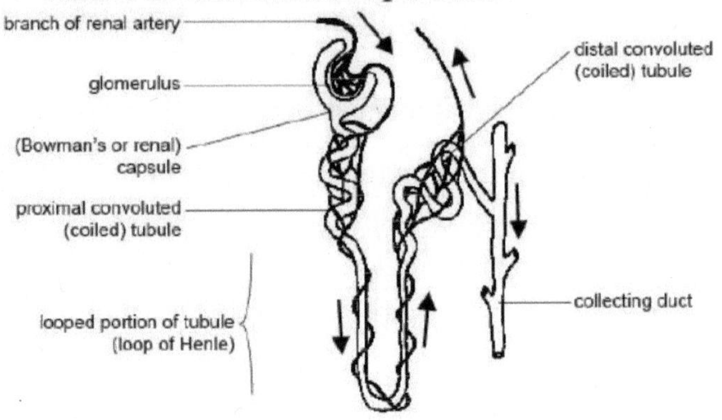
Function (i) The exchange of O_2 and CO_2 takes place between the blood of the capillaries that surround the alveoli and the gases present in the alveoli. 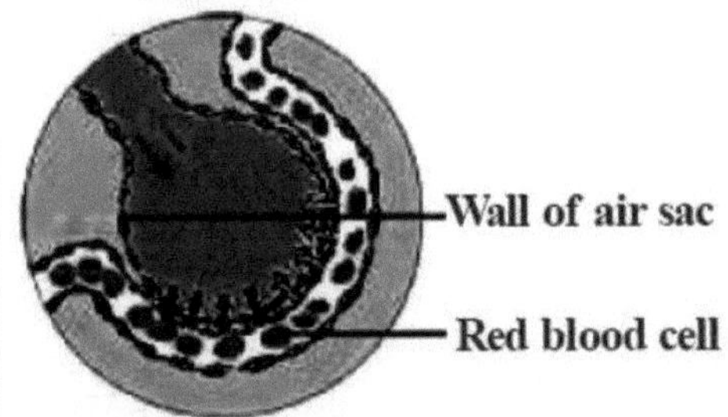 (ii) Alveoli are the site of gaseous exchange.	**Function** (i) The blood enters the kidneys through the renal artery which branches into many capillaries in the glomerulus. The water and solute are transferred to the nephron at Bowman's capsule. Then the filtrate moves through the proximal tubule and then down into the loop of henle. From henle's loop, filtrate passes into the distal tubule and then to the collecting duct. The collecting duct collects the urine from many nephrons and passes it to the ureter. During the flow of filtrate, some substances such as glucose, amino acids, and water are selectively reabsorbed. 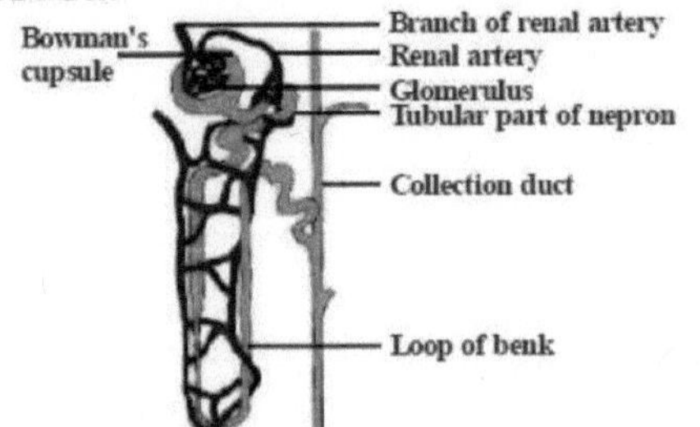 (ii) Nephrons are the basic filtration unit.

CONCEPT APPLICATION LEVEL - II

SECTION–A

1. Artifical removal of metabolic wastes from the body is called as –
(A) Ultra filteration (B) Dialysis (C) Osmoregulation (D) None of these

2. Human kidney resembles contractile vacuole of Amoeba in expelling out –
(A) Excess H_2O (B) Salts (C) Glucose (D) Urea

3. The units of a mammalian kidney are –
(A) Nephrons (B) Seminiferous tubules
(C) Uriniferous tubules (D) Ureters

4. NH_3 converted to urea in –
(A) Kidney (B) Liver (C) Spleen (D) Heart

5. Glomerular filtrate normally contain –
(A) Glucose (B) NaCl (C) Amino acids (D) All of these

6. Man is –
(A) Uricotelic (B) Ureotelic (C) Ammonotelic (D) None of these

7. Which is not excretory organ?
(A) Skin (B) Kidney (C) Liver (D) Pancreas

8. Special excretory organ is lacking in :
(A) Earthworm (B) Amoeba (C) Man (D) Insects

9. Which of the following is not a excretory product in plant –
(A) Terpentine oil (B) Latex
(C) Glucose produced during photosynthesis (D) Oxygen

10. Sweat is an excretory waste because it contains
(A) N_2 waste (B) excess H_2O (C) Salts (D) All of the above

11. Urea cycle occur in
(A) Nephron (B) Spleen (C) Pancreas (D) Liver

12. Henle's loop is short or absent in
(A) Fresh water fish (B) Birds (C) Mammals (D) All of the above

13. The white matter in a bird's dropping is
(A) $CaCO_3$ (B) $CaSO_4$ (C) Uric acid (D) Urea

14. Identify the uricotelic animal
(A) Pisces (B) Amphibia (C) Man (D) Aves

15. Organic acids which may be poisnous to a plant are stored in –
(A) Vacuoles (B) Palisade cell (C) Mesophyll (D) Xylem vassels

16. The urinary bladder of a man empties outside by means of
(A) Ureter (B) Urethra (C) Vagina (D) Glands

17. Which of the following needs large amount of water for excretion?
(A) Urea (B) Ammonia (C) Uric acid (D) Amino acids

18. Photosynthesis is maximum in which light
(A) Red light (B) Green light (C) Low light intensity (D) High light intensity

19. Cell organelle associated with conversion of light energy to chemical energy.
(A) Chloroplast (B) Mitochondria (C) Ribosome (D) ER

20. Stomata of desert plant/succulant plant are
(A) always open
(B) open during the day and close during the night
(C) Open during the night and close during the day
(D) Never open

SECTION-B

Fill in the blanks :

1. Glucose is broken down to provide energy in the form of ________.
2. The circulatory system consist of the ________, ________ and ________.
3. Plant store waste in the form of ________ and ________.
4. ________ help in ultrafilteration in kidney.

Multiple blanks :

5. Double circulatory system of blood flow includes two distinct and separate systems. This distinction is shared by most vertebrates including amphibians, _____ and mammals.In contrast, fish have a single circulation system because they lacks_______.
(A) Birds, Lungs (B) Reptiles, lungs (C) Artropoda, Lungs (D)Birds, Gills

SECTION–C
CHECK YOUR COMPATIBILITY

1. What is the importance of HCl? From where it is secreted?
2. Where & how the acidic food turns alkaline?
3. Why fishes have single circulation?
4. Why right kidney is slightly lower in position?
5. Describe the step of respiration that take place in cytoplasm.
6. What is fermentation?
7. What is the significance of large inter-cellular spaces in the plants?
8. Why cramps relieve on treatment with hot water?
9. What is residual volume? How does it helps in exchange of oxygen.
10. What is the respiratory pigment in human? What is its function?

SECTION – D
PREVIOUS YEAR'S QUESTIONS

Very Short Answer Type Questions : (One Mark)

Q.1 Write other names of the following:
(a) Alveolar sac (b) Voice box **[SAI-2015]**
Ans. (a) Air-sacs (b) Larynx.

Q.2 What is transpiration ? **[SAI-2015]**

Ans. The loss of water in the form of vapour from the aerial parts of the plant is known as transpiration.

Q.3 What is the function of valves present in auricles and ventricles ? **[SAI-2013, 2014]**

Ans. The presence of these valves ensure that blood does not flow backward when the atria or ventricles contract.

Q.4 What is meant by double circulation? **[SAI-2012, 2014]**

Ans. The circulation of blood through the heart twice during each cycle of blood circulation is known as double circulation.

Q.5 What is the function of pancreas in the human digestive system? **[SAI-2012, 2010, 2014]**

Ans. Pancreas is a large gland whose exocrine region secretes digestive enzymes (trypsin for digesting protein and pancreatic amylase for the breakdown of starch) and the endocrine region secretes hormone, insulin and glucagon.

Short Answer Type Questions : (Two Marks)

Q.6 (i) Name any two substances that are selectively reabsorbed as the urine flows along the tube.
(ii) Name the part of the excretory system in which urine is stored for sometime. **[SAI-2015]**

Ans. (i) Glucose, amino acids, salts and major amount of water.
(ii) Urinary bladder.

Q.7 Give functions of all four chambers of human heart. **[SAI-2011, 2014]**

Ans. **Functions:**
Left atrium - Receives oxygenated blood from pulmonary vein.
Right atrium - Receives deoxygenated blood from vena cava
Left ventricle - Pumps oxygenated blood to all parts of body.
Right ventricle - Pumps deoxygenated blood to lungs.

Q.8 What is the significance of residual volume of air in the lungs? **[SAI-2014]**

Ans. During the breathing cycle, when air is taken in and let out, the lungs always contain a residual volume of air so that there is sufficient time for oxygen to be absorbed and for the carbon dioxide to be released.

Q.9 What causes movement of food inside the alimentary canal? **[SAI-2014]**

Ans. The walls of alimentary canal contain muscle layers. Rhythmic contraction and relaxation of these muscles pushes the food forward. This is called peristalsis, which occurs all along the gut.

Q.10 Name the components of excretory system of human beings. **[SAI-2014]**

Ans. The excretory system of human beings includes a pair of kidney, a pair of ureters; a urinary bladder and a urethra.

Short Answer Type Questions : (Three Marks)

Q.11 Name three life processes which are essential for maintaining life and briefly explain the functioning of any one of them. **[SAI-2015]**

Ans. (a) Nutrition (b) Respiration (c) Excretion (d) Transportation (Any three)
Nutrition : It is a process of obtaining and utilising the food (nutrients), which are the source of energy. The food is needed for growth, development, synthesis of proteins and other substances needed for the maintenance of life (Metabolism).

Q.12 Define the term enzyme. State the role of saliva in human digestive system. **[SAI-2015]**

Ans. Enzymes are biological catalysts which convert complex organic food materials into smaller molecules. Saliva contains an enzyme called salivary amylase that breaks down starch which is a complex molecule to give sugar. It moistens the food, lubricates it and helps to move the food forward into alimentary canal.

Q.13 What do the following transport ?

(i) Xylem (ii) Phloem (iii) Pulmonary vein (iv) Vena cava
(v) Pulmonary artery (vi) Aorta **[SAI-2015]**

Ans. (i) Water and minerals.
(ii) Food prepared in the leaves.
(iii) Oxygenated blood from lungs to heart.
(iv) Deoxygenated blood from cells and tissues of body to heart.
(v) Deoxygenated blood from heart to lungs.
(vi) Oxygenated blood from heart to different body parts / organs.

Q.14 List the events that occur during the process of photosynthesis. **[SAI-2011, 2012]**

Ans. (a) Absorption of light energy by chlorophyll.
(b) Conversion of light energy to chemical energy and splitting of water molecules into hydrogen and oxygen.
(c) Reduction of carbon dioxide to carbohydrates.

Long Answer Type Questions : (Five Marks)

Q.15 (a) Draw a sectional view of the human heart and label on it Aorta, Right ventricle and Pulmonary veins.
(b) State the functions of the following components of transport system?
(i) Blood (ii) Lymph **[SAI-2014, 2015]**

Ans. (a)

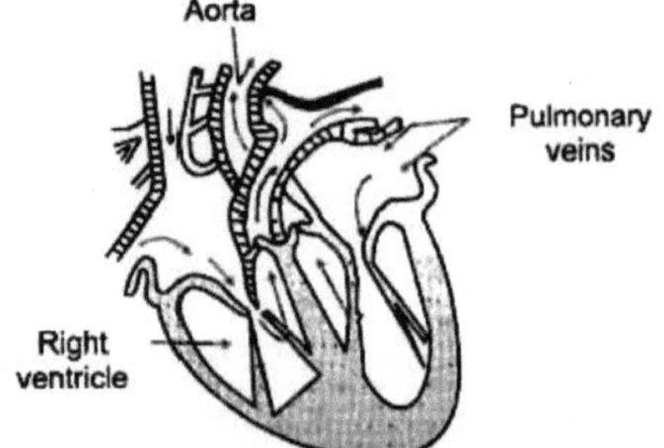

(b) (i) **Blood:** It transports food, oxygen and waste materials in human body.
(ii) **Lymph:** It carries digested and absorbed fat from intestine and drains excess fluid from extracellular space back into the blood.

Q.16 What are stomata? What functions do they perform? With the help of a diagram explain opening and closing of stomata. **[SAI-2014, 2015]**

Ans. Stomata are the tiny pores present on the surface of leaves.
Functions of stomata: (i) Exchange of gases, (ii) Transpiration

- Opening and closing of stomata occurs due to turgor changes in guard cells. When guard cells are turgid, stomatal pore is open while in flaccid conditions, the aperture closes.

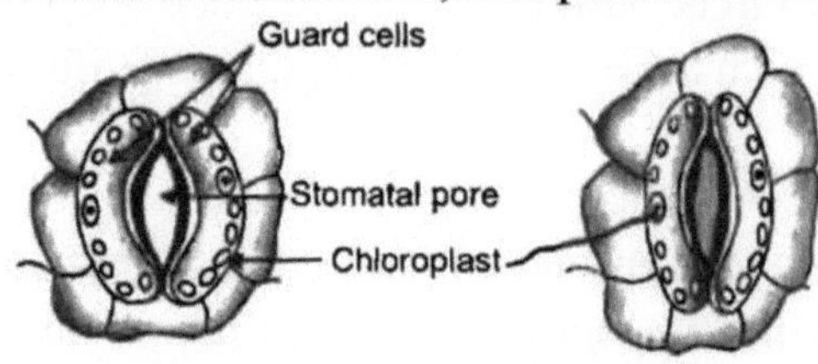

(*a*) Open stomatal pore (*b*) Closed stomatal pore

SECTION – E
UNDERSTANDING BASED QUESTIONS

Q.1 When we breathe out, why does the air passage not collapse? **[SAI-2014, 2015]**

Ans. Because trachea (wind pipe) is lined by rings of cartilage which ensure that the air passage does not collapse.

Q.2 Why is it necessary to separate oxygenated and deoxygenated blood in mammals and birds ? **[SAI-2014]**

Ans. They have high energy requirement for maintaining their body temperature. This is possible only if oxygenated and deoxygenated blood remain separated.

Q.3 Why is diffusion insufficient to meet the oxygen requirements of multicellular organisms like humans ? **[SAI-2015]**

Ans. In the multicellular organisms, all the cells may not be in direct contact with the surrounding environment. Therefore, the diffusion is insufficient to meet the oxygen requirements in them. Instead, they need specialised organs for breathing and exchange of gases.

Q.4 (a) In which forms nitrogen is taken by plants ?
(b) Which type of nutrition is present in bread mould? **[SAI-2013, 2014]**

Ans. (a) Nitrogen is taken-up from the soil in the form of inorganic nitrates or nitrites. Or it is taken-up as organic compounds which have been prepared by bacteria from atmospheric nitrogen.
(b) Saprophytic (Heterotrophic) nutrition : They breakdown the food material outside the body and then absorb it.

Q.5 How does aerobic respiration differ from anaerobic respiration? **[SAI-2015]**

Ans.

Aerobic respiration	Anaerobic respiration
1. Oxygen is utilised for the breakdown of respiratory substrate.	1. Oxygen is not required.
2. It takes place in cytoplasm (glycolysis) and inside mitochondria (Krebs cycle).	2. It takes place in cytoplasm only.
3. End products are carbon dioxide and water.	3. End products are lactic acid or ethanol and carbon dioxide.
4. More energy is released.	4. Less energy is released.

Q.6 Why do fishes have two chambered heart and reptiles have three chambered heart? **[SAI-2014]**

Ans. Division of heart depends on the energy needs by an organism. Since these animals do not require high energy to maintain their body temperature thus, they have two and three chambers respectively to meet their minimum energy requirements. These animals tolerate some mixing of the oxygenated and deoxygenated blood streams. Due to these reasons, the body temperature of these aniinals depends on the temperature of the environment.

CONCEPT APPLICATION LEVEL - III

SECTION-A

Multiple choice question with one correct answers :

1. Which among them is not correct equation of an anabolic process in plants
   (A) $C_6H_{12}O_6 + 6O_2 \rightarrow 6CO_2 + 6H_2O$
   (B) $6CO_2 + 6H_2O \rightarrow C_6H_{12}O_6 + 6O_2$
   (C) $6CO_2 + 12H_2O \rightarrow C_6H_{12}O_6 + 6O_2 + 6H_2O$
   (D) All of these

2. Organelle responsible for anabolic process of food production in plant.
   (A) Mitochondria (B) Peroxisome (C) Ribosome (D) Plastids

3. A major metabolic process taking place in germinating seed to
   (A) Photosynthesis (B) Absorption of water
   (C) Absorption of mineral (D) Respiration

4. Catabolism is
   (A) Anabolism first than metabolism (B) Breakdown of the product of anabolism
   (C) Formation of the product in a cell (D) All of the above

5. Growth in a plant is because of
   (A) More anabolism than catabolism (B) More catabolism than anabolism
   (C) Equal amount of anabolism and catabolism (D) More energy consumption

6. Photosynthetically active radiation (PAR) represents the following range of wavelength
   (A) 400 – 700 nm (B) 500 – 600 nm (C) 450 – 950 nm (D) 340–450 nm

7. In chlorophyll which metal is present?
   (A) Mn (B) Mo (C) Mg (D) S

8. Photolysis of water take place in
   (A) Absorption (B) Transpiration (C) Respiration (D) Photosynthesis

9. Photolysis is
   (A) Another name for photosynthesis (B) Another name for respiration
   (C) Breakdown of glucose (D) Breakdown of water

10. During light reactions the following molecules are formation
    (A) ATP (B) ATP & NADPH (C) NADPH (D) None

11. Dark reaction of photosynthesis
(A) Takes place in dim light
(B) Takes place both in light and dark
(C) Is termed as dark reaction because it is inhibited by light
(D) Utilizes the assimilatory power formed in light reaction

12. In which form is food transported in plants
(A) Sucrose (B) Fructose (C) Glucose (D) Lactose

13. Some plant absorb CO_2 at night. They are
(A) Water plant (B) Land plant (C) Desert plant (D) Both (A)&(B)

14. Magnesium is constituent of which pigment?
(A) Florigen (B) Chlorophyll (C) Haemoglobin (D) Enzyme

15. In photosynthesis
(A) CO_2 is reduced while H_2O oxidized (B) CO_2 is oxidized white H_2O reduced
(C) CO_2 and H_2O are oxidized (D) CO_2 & H_2O are reduced

16. In chloroplast, chlorophyll is present in the
(A) Stroma (B) Outer membrane (C) Inner membrane (D) Thylakoids

17. Phenomenon which converts light energy into chemical energy is
(A) Respiration (B) Photosynthesis (C) Transpiration (D) None of these

18. Chlorophyll in chloroplast is located in
(A) Grana (B) Pyrenoid (C) Stroma (D) None of these

SECTION-B

Assertion & Reason :

Instructions: In the following questions as Assertion (A) is given followed by a Reason (R). Mark your responses from the following options.

(A) Both Assertion and Reason are true and Reason is the correct explanation of 'Assertion'
(B) Both Assertion and Reason are true and Reason is not the correct explanation of 'Assertion'
(C) Assertion is true but Reason is false
(D) Assertion is false but Reason is true

1. **Assertion :** Oxygen is absorbed by different organs in different organism.
Reason : All these organs have structure that increase surface area.

2. **Assertion :** It would take 3 year for a molecule of oxygen to get to our toes from our lungs.
Reason : Diffusion is movement from high to low concentration.

SECTION-C

Match the following (one to one) :

Column-I and **column-II** contains **four** entries each. Entries of column-I are to be matched with some entries of column-II. Only One entries of column-I may have the matching with the some entries of column-II and one entry of column-II Only one matching with entries of column-I

1.

Column I		**Column II**
(A)	Bronchiole	(P) Circulation
(B)	Vena cava	(Q) Absorption
(C)	Glomerulus	(R) Respiration
(D)	Villi	(S) Excretion

Match the following (one to many) :

Column-I and **column-II** contains **four** entries each. Entries of column-I are to be matched with some entries of column-II. One or more than one entries of column-I may have the matching with the some entries of column-II and one entry of column-II may have one or more than one matching with entries of column-I

2.

Column I		**Column II**
(A)	Lactic acid	(P) Aerobic respiration
(B)	Ethanol	(Q) Anaerobic respiration
(C)	CO_2	(R) Photosynthesis
(D)	O_2	(S) Transpiration

SECTION-D

Comprehension :

Photosynthesis is a process by which green plant make there own food in the presence of sunlight, water, CO_2 and chlorophyll. If we keep a water plant in a beaker, inverted by a funnel and a test tube placed over having water than we can see bubble of gas accumulated at the bottom of the test tube. This gas down ward displaces water.

Q.1 Name the process by which this gas is produced
(A) Respiration (B) Transpiration (C) Photolysis (D) None

Q.2 Which among them is not an aquatic plant?
(A) Hydrilla (B) Hydra (C) Vallisneria (D) Lotus

Q.3 Gas that helps in formation of ozone comes out during.
(A) Respiration (B) Photosynthesis (C) Absorption (D) Translocation

******

ANSWER KEY

Try yourself :

1.	B	2.	C	3.	B	4.	B	5.	A
6.	C	7.	B	8.	C	9.	B	10.	A
11.	D	12.	A	13.	B	14.	A	15.	A
16.	B	17.	B	18.	D	19.	B	20.	D
21.	A	22.	C	23.	B	24.	C	25.	A
26.	A	27.	A	28.	B	29.	C	30.	A
31.	A	32.	D						

CONCEPT APPLICATION LEVEL - II

SECTION–A

1.	B	2.	A	3.	A	4.	B	5.	D
6.	B	7.	D	8.	B	9.	C	10.	D
11.	D	12.	A	13.	C	14.	D	15.	A
16.	B	17.	B	18.	A	19.	A	20.	C

SECTION-B

1.	ATP	2.	Heart, Blood & blood vessel	3.	Gum and resin
4.	Bowman capsules	5.	(A) Birds, Lungs		

CONCEPT APPLICATION LEVEL - III

SECTION-A

1.	A	2.	D	3.	D	4.	B	5.	A
6.	A	7.	C	8.	D	9.	D	10.	B
11.	D	12.	A	13.	C	14.	B	15.	A
16.	D	17.	B	18.	A				

SECTION-B

1.	B	2.	B

SECTION-C

1. A–R, B–P, C–S, D–Q
2. A–Q, B–Q, C–PQR, D–PR

SECTION-D

1.	C	2.	B	3.	B

2 CONTROL AND COORDINATION

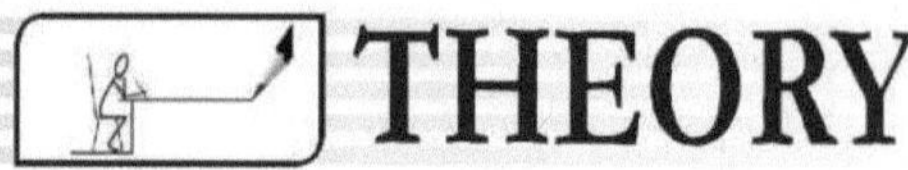

THEORY

INTRODUCTION

Living organisms respond and react to their external environment. The linking together of various activities in the living organism is known as **coordination**. The process of co-ordination must be carefully **controlled.**

- Plants do not have any special structure for perception of stimuli. In plants control and coordination is performed by chemical substances known as plant hormones or phytohormone. Phytohormones are of five types namely Auxins, Gibberellins, Cytokinins, Abscissic Acid (ABA) and Ethylene.
- Multicellular animals except sponge have specialized cells called neurons for responding to stimuli. Neuron or nerve cell is the structural and functional unit of the nervous system. Nervous system includes brain, spinal cord and nerves. Nervous system and Endocrine or hormonal system control and coordinate body functions in animals.

CONTROL AND COORDINATION IN PLANTS

- Plants lack nervous system and muscles so they relay on chemical or hormonal control.

Stimulus and Response:

- Stimulus is the change in the external or internal environment of an organism that provokes a physiological and behavioral change in the organism. The changes thus caused are termed as **response.**
- **Tropism :** Movement of plant towards the direction of stimulus is called **tropism**. Eg. Bending of shoot towards light is called positive phototropism. Root of plants show negative phototropism. Downward movement is in response to gravitational force is called geotropism. Roots of plants shows positive geotropisms, stems show negative geotropism.
- Other movements in plants which are caused by external stimuli but are not directional are called **nastic movements** (such as in touch-me-not plant).

Type of Plant Movements

- Plants show two types of movements – one dependent on growth and other independent of growth.

Plant Movement	
Nastic (Non-directional)	**Tropic (Directional)**
Rapid response to non directional stimuli (eg temperature)	Slow response to directional stimuli.
It is reversible as independent of growth	Related to growth so irrevesible
eg. Movement in Mimosa pudica on touching (thigmonastic)	eg. Bending of shoot towards light (phototropic)

1. Non-directional or Nastic movement :

- The movement of a plant in response to an external stimuli in which the direction of response is not determined by the direction of stimulus is called nastic movement.
- The nastic movements of plants are induced by stimuli such as heat, light, touch (or contact) etc.
- There are several types of nastic movement: They are:

(i) **Photonasty.** Plants show sleep movements according to the day and night pattern of the sun light. There is a circardian rhythm which is followed by the biological clock on earth.

(ii) **Thermonasty.** This is movement in response to temperature changes e.g. flowers of tulips open at high temperature and close at low temperature.

(iii) **Nyctinasty.** This is the response of a plant to darkness. e.g. folding and unfolding of leaflets in *Oxalis*, opening and closing of stomata.

(iv) **Siesmonasty.** This is plant movement brought about by touch or the shock generated by touch e.g. ***Mimosa pudica***. [Thigmo-nastic movement (Thigmo = touch, Nastic = non directional), growth independent].

(v) **Hyponasty.** These are movements or upward bending of leaves and other plant parts due to growth of lower part of a plant.

Do you Know :

Some plants such as Snapdragons are described as night-neutral or day neutral. Their flowering does not depend on the night's length.

---

2. Directional or Tropic Movement :

- It is the directional growth or movement of plant organ in response to an external stimulus. Thus, growth dependent movement.
- Growth towards the stimulus is positive tropism and growth away from the stimulus is negative tropism.
- Tropic movements are classified as follows, depending on the type of stimulus causing it:

(i) **Phototropism** is the movement of part of the plant in response to light. The main factor responsible for it is differential movement of Auxin concentration towards shade area when unidirectional light is provided. So, the part which is in shade grows more and particular part of plant tilt towards source of light.

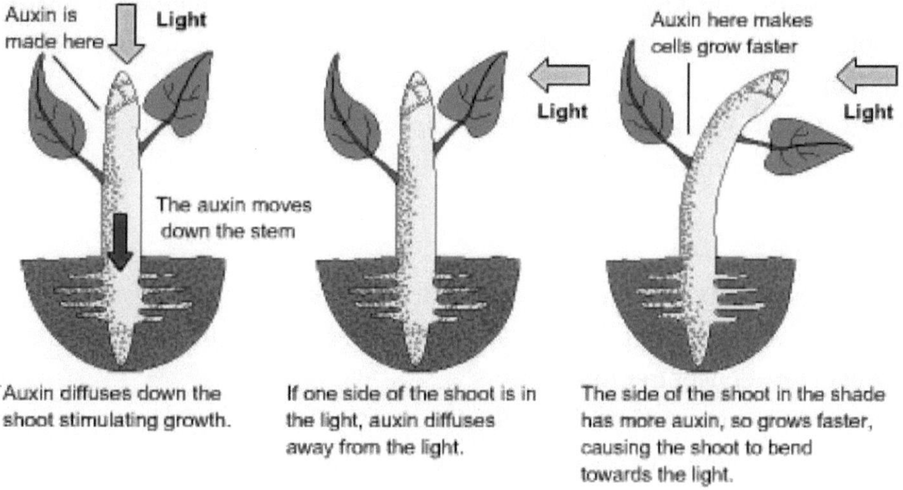

(ii) **Geotropism** is the upward growth of shoots (Negative) and downward growth of roots (Positive) in response to the pull of earth or gravity. It is due to accumulation of Auxin in lower half.

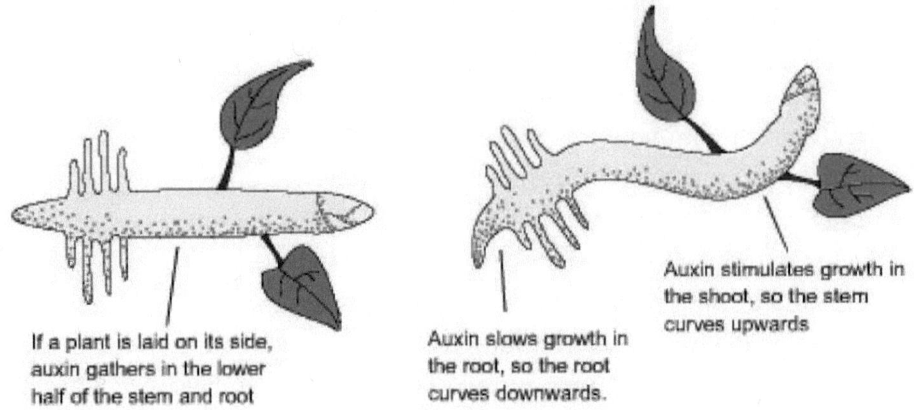

(iii) **Hydrotropism** is the movement of a part of the plant in response to water. It is stronger as compared to geotropism as shown in the figure that root denies gravity to ensure water availability.

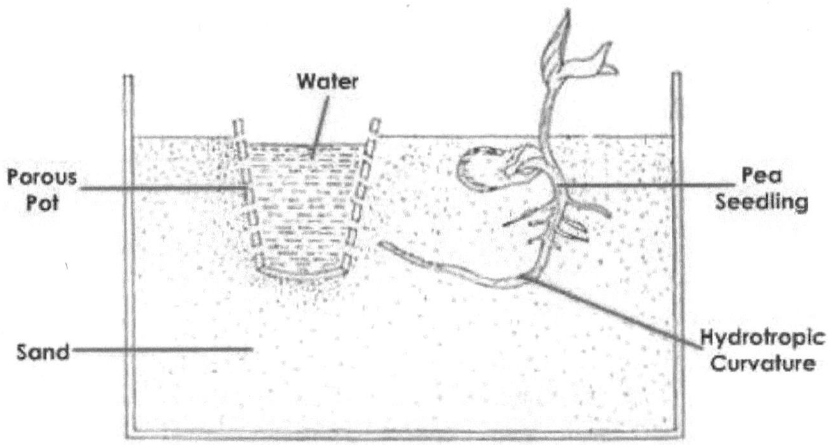

(iv) **Chemotropism** is the movement of a part of the plant in response to a chemical stimulus. If the plant part shows movement or growth towards the chemical, it is called **positive chemotropism** and if the plant part shows movement or growth away from the chemical, it is called **negative chemotropism**.
For example, the growth the pollen tube towards a chemical which is produced by cells of ovule during the process of fertilization in a flower.

PLANT HORMONE

- **Plant Hormones or Phytohormones** can be defined as chemical substances which are produced naturally in plants and are capable of translocation and regulate one or more physiological processes when present in low concentration.
- Plant hormones help to coordinate growth, development and responses to the environment.
- They are synthesized at places away from where they act and simply diffuse to the area of action.

Types of Phytohormones

- The major types of plant hormones that are involved in the control and coordination are as follows :

(1) Auxins : Indole Acetic Acid (IAA) is major Auxin in plants.

Important function :

(i) Responsible for tropic movement. Plants bend towards sunlight (Positive Phototropism).

(ii) Help in increasing length of plant as these are synthesized at the tip of roots and shoots. Cell elongation is the primary and chief function of auxin in plants. By removing tips we can make the plants bushy. As apical bud suppresses growth of lateral buds in plants. It is called **apical dominance.**

(iii) These induce parthenocarpy to obtain seedless fruits eg. seed less grapes, papaya etc.

(iv) Prevent falling of unripen fruits.

(v) Help in removal of weeds eg. 2, 4–D.

(2) Gibberellins :

(i) These stimulate the elongation of stem particularly **at the internodal region.**

(ii) These induce germination of dormant seeds.

(iii) Help in removing genetic dwarfism.

(iv) Help in flowering and development of fruits.

(3) Cytokinins :

(i) These compounds are synthesized in the seeds and the roots of the plants.

(ii) These promote cell division by activating DNA synthesis and protein synthesis.

(iii) They are present in large concentration in areas of rapid cell division (such as fruits and seeds).

(iv) Break dormancy.

(v) Delay senescence.

(4) Abscisic acid (ABA) :

(i) Commonly known as **stress hormone** because the production of hormone is stimulated by drought, water logging and other adverse environmental conditions.

(ii) It reverses the promotory effects of Auxins and gibberellins.

(iii) **Abscisic acid** is primarily a **growth Inhibitor** responsible for wilting of leaves. It is found in leaves, dormant seeds, buds and other parts of the plant.

(iv) ABA promotes abscission of leaves, flowers and fruits.

(v) It also promotes the **senescence of leaves**.

(vi) Helps in reducing transpiration rates by closing stomata.

(5) Ethylene

(i) Ethylene is a **gaseous plant hormone** that stimulates transverse growth but retards the longitudinal one.

(ii) It is formed in almost all plant parts – roots, leaves, flowers and seeds.

(iii) **Ethylene promotes** fruit growth and its ripening.

(iv) Normally reduces flowering in plants except pineapple.

(v) It behaves as growth inhibitor.

Character	Auxin	GA	CK	ABA	C_2H_4
Stem elongation	↑↑	↑↑	No effect or ↓↓	No effect	↓↓
Cell division & cell elongation	↑↑	↑↑	↑↑ with auxin	↓↓	No. effect
Root initiation	↑↑	No effect or inhibit	↓↓	No effect	↑↑
Seed germination	↓↓	↑↑	↑↑	↓↓	↑↑
Seed germination	↓↓	↑↑	↑↑	↓↓	↑↑
Dormancy	maintain	Break	Break	maintain	Break
Abscission	↓↓	No effect	↓↓	↑↑	↑↑
Senescence	delay	No effect	delay	Promote	Promote
Apical dominance	↑↑	No effect	↓↓	No effect	No effect
Parthenocarpy	↑↑	↑↑	No effect	No effect	No effect

PHOTOPERIODISM

Flowering and germination of seeds in plants is controlled by duration of day light (photoperiod). This phenomenon is called photoperiodism.

On the basis of length of photoperiod requirements of plants, they have been classified into.

(i) Short day plants — Xanthium, Sugarcane

(ii) Long day plants — Spinach, Radish

(iii) Day neutral plants — Cotton, Sunflower

Response of plants to photoperiodic stimulus is due to a specialized pigment **phytochrome**.

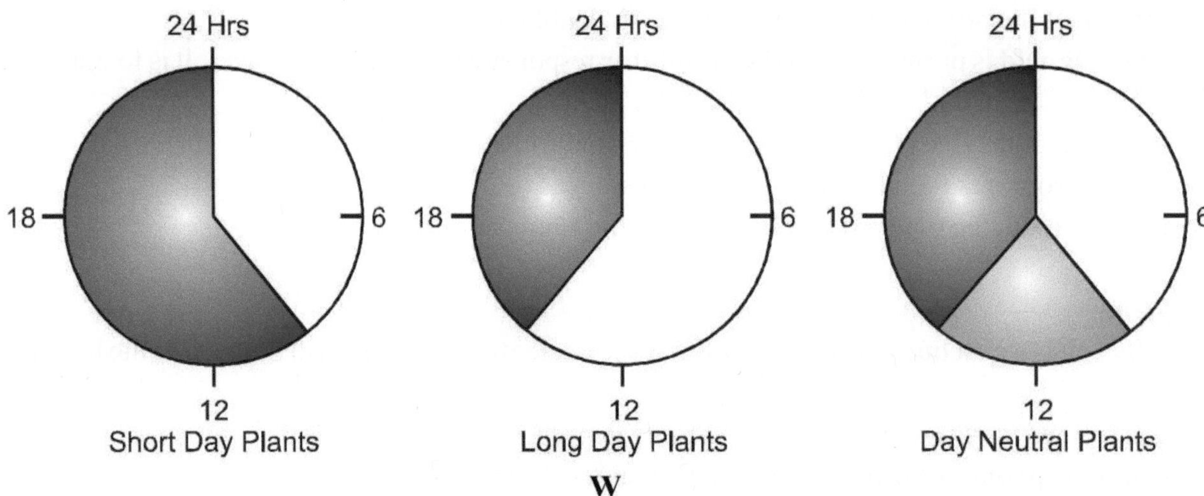

W

Requirement of light and dark periods during 24 hours for flowering in short day, long day and day neutral plants.

CONTROL AND COORDINATION IN ANIMALS

Animals receive external information through specialized structure called sense organs (receptors). These are photoreceptors for light, phonoreceptors for sound and olfactoreceptors for smell. Control and coordination is achieved by two systems (a) nervous system (b) endocrine system.

A. NERVOUS SYSTEM AND SENSE ORGANS OF ANIMALS

- In animals, control and co-ordination is achieved with the help of nervous and muscular tissues. Nervous system is made up of specialized cells called **neurons**.

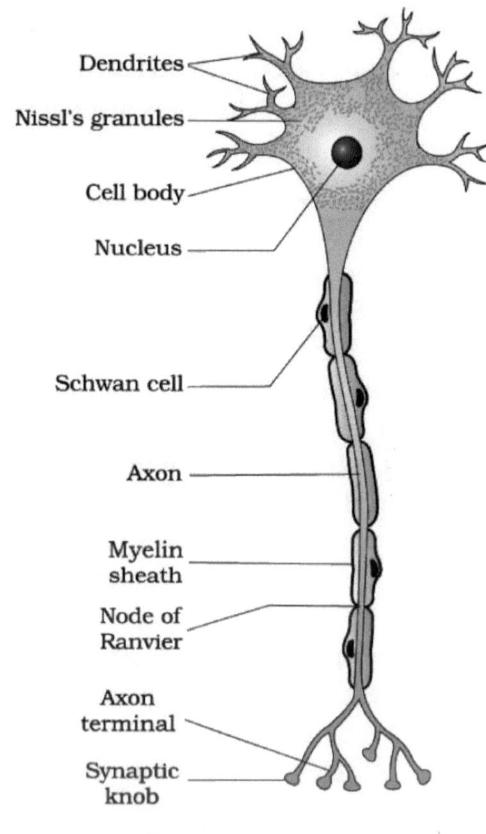

Structure of a neuron

Structure of neuron

- A neuron (nerve cell) consists of cyton and processes :

(a) Cell body / Cyton / Soma

- **Cyton** or cell body has a central nucleus and surrounding cytoplasm.
- Around the nucleus there are granules called **Nissles granules,** which are made up of RNA and Protein (exact function unknown, they are believed to convert a nerve impulse into an electrical impluse). It transfers impulse to axon.

(b) Two types of processes namely dendrites and axon.

Dendrites:

- These are hair like processes connected to the Cyton through dendrone.
- They receive sensation or stimulus, which may be physical, chemical, mechanical or electrical.
- The information received at dendrite tip sets up a chemical reaction that creates an electric impulse.
- This impulse travels from dendrite to cell body

Axon

- It is the longer part of the neuron.
- It transmits the impulse from Cyton to the tip of the axon called **axon bulb.**
- The plasma membrane of an axon may be covered by a sheath of lipid and protein called the **myelin sheath.**
- The sheath is formed by the **Schwann cells**, and is broken into constrictions called the **nodes of Ranvier.**
- The ending of axon is called **synaptic terminals or nerve endings.**
- The impulse on reaching terminal releases some chemicals or neuro-hormones i.e. Acetyl Choline (Ach) or glutamic acid which crosses the synapse (The physical gap between a synaptic terminal and the dendrite of another neuron or an effector cell) and transfer impulses to next neurons.
- These chemicals start a similar electrical impulse in dendrite of next neuron and in same manner impulses are transmitted to effectors, such as muscles (Neuromuscular junction) and/or glands.

Knowledge Enhancer :

Synapse is the point of contact between the terminal branches of the axon of a neuron with one dendrites of another neuron. Here the nerve impules "jumps" into the next neuron. This is a chemical process. As the impulse reaches the terminal end of an axon, a chemical acetylcholine

or glutamic acid is released. This chemical sets a new impulse in the dentrites of the adjacent (next) neuron. The chemical is soon broken down by an enzyme to make the synapse ready for the next tranmission.

Do you Know :

Impulse is an electrical disturbance received by the dendrite and passed through the cyton to the axon. Messages are transmitted in the form of electrical impulses along the fibre of the neurons. It flows only unidirectionally.

- A nerve may terminate in one of the given three ways :
  (i) Synapse
  (ii) Neuromates junction / Neuroglandular junction
  (iii) Sensory nerve ending

Types of Nervous System in Animals

- In all **vertebrates** including humans the nervous system may be divided into the **Central nervous system and peripheral nervous system.** Peripheral nervous system may be somatic or autonomous.

(A) **Central nervous system (CNS)** consisting of brain and spinal cord.There are **12 pairs of cranial** and **31 pairs of spinal** nerves in humans.

(B) **Peripheral nervous system (PNS)** consisting of cranial nerves and spinal nerves. It connects CNS to the body organs.PNS may be somatic and autonomic as defined below:

- PNS that connects CNS and voluntary muscles is **Somatic** and that connects CNS to involuntary muscles is **Autonomic Nervous System (ANS).**

Autonomic Nervous System (ANS) may be further of two types

(A) **Sympathetic**:The sympathetic division typically functions when quick responses to stimulus is require. It dialates pupil, Inhibits flow of saliva and contract bladder but acclerates heart beat.

(B) **Parasympathetic**:The parasympathetic division functions with actions that do not require immediate reaction.It constricts pupil, increases flow of saliva, relaxes bladder but slows down heart beat.

- Sympathetic and parasympathetic divisions are typically antagonistic to each other. The sympathetic division work as the accelerator and the parasympathetic division works as a brake.
- A useful acronym to summarize the functions of the autonomous nervous system is STUDD (salivation, tear, urination, digestion and defecation).

FUNCTIONS OF AUTONOMIC NERVOUS SYSTEM		
Organ	**Function of sympathetic system**	**Function of parasympathetic system**
Heart	Accelerates heart beat	Slows heart beat
Arteries	Constricts arteries & raises blood pressure	Dilates arteries & lowers blood pressure
Urinary bladder	Relaxes bladder	Constricts bladder
Muscles of iris	Dilate pupil	Constricts pupil

The arrangement of the nerves of the body into vertebrate nervous system

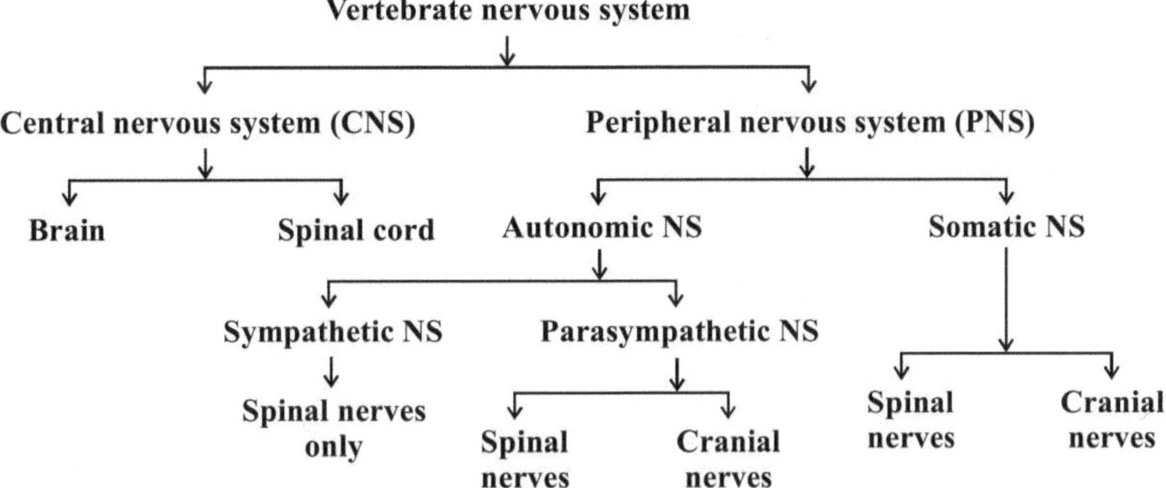

SENSE ORGANS / RECEPTORS

- Information from environment is gained by specialized tips of the nerve cells or receptors. These receptors are located in our sense organs like
  (i) Photoreceptors for light eg. eye.
  (ii) Phonoreceptors for sound eg. ear.
  (iii) Olfactory receptors for smell eg. nose.
  (iv) Gustatory receptor for taste eg. tongue.
  (v) Tango receptor for touch eg. skin.

REFLEX ACTION AND REFLEX ARC

- **Reflex action** is a spontaneous, automatic, mechanical response to a stimulus.
- It is involuntary response of effectors (glands or muscles) to stimuli, **mediated by spinal cord.** (The **spinal cord** is a long, thin, tubular bundle of nervous tissue. It is part of CNS mainly concerned with reflex action.)
- Thinking is a complex activity which involves a complicated interaction of many nerve impulses from many neurons.
- This interaction requires time. In case of urgent situation like touching hot plate, body needs quick system which takes immediate action to minimize damage.
- Such system is reflex system and it is mediated by spinal cord. (**Ian Pavlov** is regarded as the father of reflex action).
- Nerve from all over the body meets in bundle in spinal cord on their way to brain.
- Since spinal cord is the first point where nerves meet each other, so reflex action is mediated by spinal cord.
- After action is complete, the input information reaches brain. Brain has no direct role in reflex action.

Examples of reflex action

- Withdrawal of hand when it touches hot object.
- Knee jerk reflex (on tapping Patella leg move forward).
- Constriction of pupil when strong light is flashed.
- Sneezing, coughing and yawning.

- Path followed by an impulse in reflex action is known as **reflex arc**. Reflex always travels in one direction in the following sequence

Stimulus → Receptor organ → Sensory nerves → spinal cord → Motor nerve → Effector organ → Response

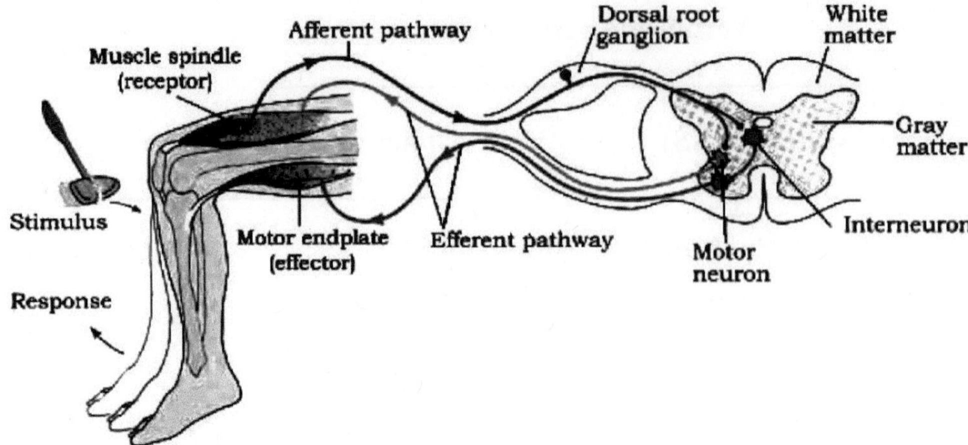

Diagrammatic presentation of reflex action (showing knee jerk reflex)

Significance of Reflex Action

(i) It enables the body to give quick responses to threatening stimuli and thus protects our body.

(ii) It helps to minimize the overloading of brain.

(iii) Thinking process of brain is not fast enough.

(iv) Many lower groups of animals have very little or none of the complex neuron network needed for thinking. In them the reflex arcs have evolved as efficient ways of functioning in the absence of true thought processes.

Do you know?

- As per definition reflex actions are purely instinctive. Such reflex are **unconditioned reflex**.
- Ian Pavlon however demonstrated that some reflex can be learnt by training. Such reflexes are termed as **Conditioned reflex.**

HUMAN BRAIN

- It is the highest coordinating centre in the body. Complex processes like thinking, memory etc. are concerned to brain.

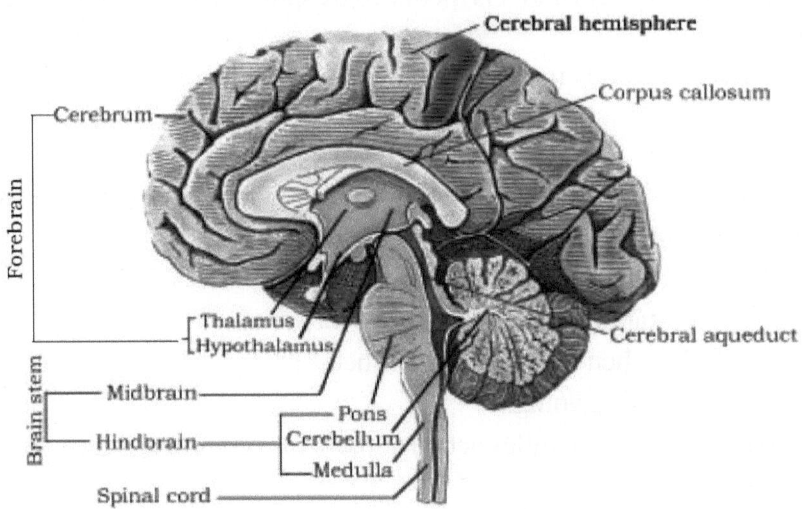

The brain is broadly divided into three regions : Fore-brain, mid-brain and hind-brain.

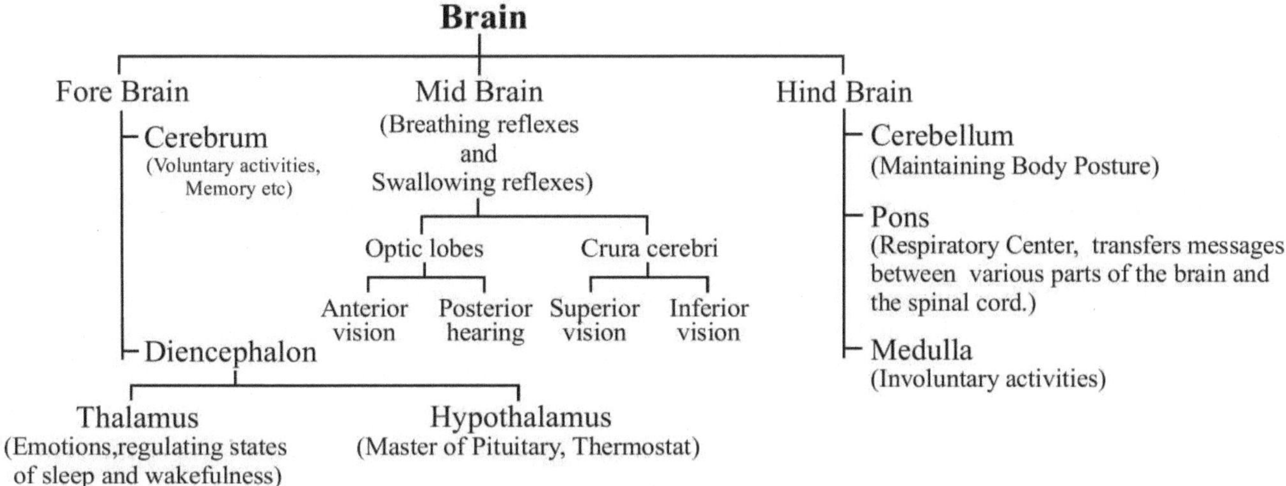

I. FORE-BRAIN

Its includes Cerebrum and Diencephalon (Thalamus and hypothalamus) .

A. Cerebrum

- The cerebrum is the largest part of the human brain, associated with higher brain function such as thought and action.
- The cerebrum is divided into four sections, called "lobes": the frontal lobe, parietal lobe, occipital lobe, and temporal lobe.

(a) Occipital lobe is the regions for sight, i.e., visual reception.

(b) Temporal lobe is the region for hearing, i.e. auditory reception.

(c) Frontal lobe is the region for speech, facial muscular activities and higher mental activities.

(d) Parietal lobe is the region for taste, smell, touch and conscious association.

- The cerebrum has **sensory areas** where information is received from the sense organs called **receptors**.
- Similarly, cerebrum has **motor areas** from where instructions are sent to the various muscles of the body called **effectors** to do the various jobs.
- **Areas of association** are present in cerebral cortex.
- They are neither sensory nor motor.
- They receive information from sensory areas and is involved in "higher" functions such as perception, thoughts and decision-making, etc.

B. Diencephalon : Smallest part of brain

Epithalamus : roof of brain

- **Thalamus**

  It is essentially a relay station that receives sensory information and passes it on to the cerebral cortex. It is related to emotions and controlling state of wakefulness and sleep.

- **Hypothalamus**

  It is master of master endocrine gland which is mainly responsible for maintaining body temperature **(Thermostat)**. It also regulates desires, Food and Water Intake, Sleep & Wake Cycle etc.

II. MID-BRAIN

It connects the fore-brain to hind-brain. It controls reflex movement of the head, neck and trunk in response to visual and auditory stimuli. It is also related to audio and visual response.

III. HIND-BRAIN

It consists of three centers called Cerebellum, Pons and Medulla oblongata.

- **Cerebellum** lies at the roof of the hind-brain. This region controls the coordination of body movements and posture. It is **second largest** part of brain.
- **Pons** lies just above the medulla and take part in regulating respiration.
- **Medulla oblongata** lies at the floor of the hind-brain and continues into the spinal cord. It is also the regulating centre for swallowing, coughing, sneezing and vomiting. Medulla contains respiratory center.
- Thus, pons and medulla both regulate involuntary activities of body.
- It comes out of cranial cavity through foramen magnum and after coming out it is called **spinal cord.**

DIFFERENT PARTS OF BRAIN AND THEIR FUNCTIONS		
PARTS OF BRAIN	**SUB-DIVISIONS**	**FUNCTIONS**
1. Fore Brain	**(a)** Olfactory lobes	Sense of smell.
	(b) Cerebrum (largest and most complex part of brain).	Centre for memory and intelligence.
	(c) Diencephalon : Thalamus & Hypothalamus	Centre for emotions, sweating, fatigue, sleep, thirst, pain, hunger, body temperature, fear etc.
2. Mid Brain	Cerebral peduncles or Crura cerebri (fibre tracts)	Receive sensory impulses from eyes, ears and muscles of head. Relay impulses back and forth between the cerebrum, cerebellum, pons and medulla.
3. Hindbrain	**a)** Cerebellum	Controls the rapid muscular activities such as running, typing etc. Controls body posture
	b) Pons varolii	Relay impulse between medulla oblongata and upper parts of brain. It contains centres that work with those of medulla oblongata to regulate respiratory rate.
	c) Medulla oblongata	**i)** It controls various involuntary movements of the body. **ii)** It has a respiratory centre to regulate respiration. **iii)** It has reflex centre for swallowing, vomiting, peristalsis, salivation, coughing, sneezing etc.

Knowledge Enhancer :

(i) Electroencephalogram :

It is graph made by an instrument called encephalograph that records the waves of the brain. The minute electrical waves produced by the nerve cells of the brain are transmitted to the instrument, which amplifies and records them on strip of paper.

(ii) Spinal Cord :

It lies in the mid-dorsal region along the longitudial axis of the body. It is a slender, cylindrical structure, about 45 cm long, originating from medulla oblongata and extending downwards upto the lumber region. It then extends to the end of vetebral column as fibrous connective called filum terminals. Spinal cord is enclosed in the vertebral column, which protects it. Internally, the spinal cord possesses a narrow fluid-filled cavity called central canal. Spinal cord is also covered by three meninges, like the brain, in between which is the cerebrospinal fluid.

Spinal cord acts as a centre for reflex actions, thus, reduces brain's work. It also conducts sensory and motor impulses to and from the brain.

Thirty–one pairs of spinal nerves arise from the spinal cord and twelve pairs of nerves arise from the brain.

Protection of Central Nervous System (Brain and Spinal Cord)

- Owing to function and importance of Central Nervous System it is well protected inside the body.
- Brain is protected inside brain box or cranium.
- Brain is covered by layers known as meninges (Outer Dura-mater, Arachnoid, and Pia-mater)
- Spinal cord is protected by Vertebral column & meninges.
- Brain has grey matter on the outer side and white matter in the centre while the spinal cord has the reverse i.e., grey matter in the central core and white matter on the outer side.

How does the Nervous Tissue cause Action on Effector (Muscles).

- The nervous tissue collects information from receptors and sends it to the brain (CNS), brain processes information and makes decision.
- Decision is conveyed to muscles for action.
- When a nerve impulse reaches the muscles, the muscle fibers move by changing the shape of the muscle cells with the help of special proteins (actin and myosin).
- This process require certain chemical massenger (Neuro-hormones) to transmit impulses to muscles and also ATP and Ca^{++} ions. Impulse is transmitted in electrochemical form.
- **The overall pathway is:**
  Nervous tissue → **Collect information → Transfer information → Brain Process information → Interpretation → Action (By muscle & glands)**

B. HORMONES IN ANIMALS

Chemical Messengers

- Hormones are the chemical substances which coordinate and control the activities of living organisms and also their growth.
- The term hormone was introduced by **Bayliss** and **Starling**. Hormones are chemically made up of proteins or lipids.

Characteristics and Functions of Hormones

(i) Hormones are the secretions of endocrine (ductless) glands.

(ii) They are poured directly into the blood and carried through out the body by blood circulatory system.

(iii) Hormones have their effect at the sites different from the sites of there origin. So, they are also called **'chemical messengers'**.

(iv) They act on specific tissues or organs called **'target organs'** or **'target site'**.

(v) They coordinate the activities of the body and also its growth.

(vi) They are secreted in extremely minute quantities.

(vii) Hormones are non-nutrient chemical which act as inter-cellular messengers.

DIFFERENCES BETWEEN EXOCRINE & ENDOCRINE GLANDS.		
S.NO.	EXOCRINE GLANDS	ENDOCRINE GLANDS
1.	Exocrine glands have ducts.	Endocrine glands are ductless.
2.	These glands discharge their secretions into the ducts.	These glands discharge their secretions directly into the blood.
3.	These glands are present near the site of action. **Examples :** Sweat and oil glands of skin, salivary glands, etc.	These glands are present far away from the site of action.**e.g.**Pituitary, thyroid, hypothalamus, etc.

ENDOCRINE GLANDS

- These are the structures or group of cells or tissue which manufacture hormones and secrete them directly into the bloodstream to act at distant sites in the body known as target organs or cells.

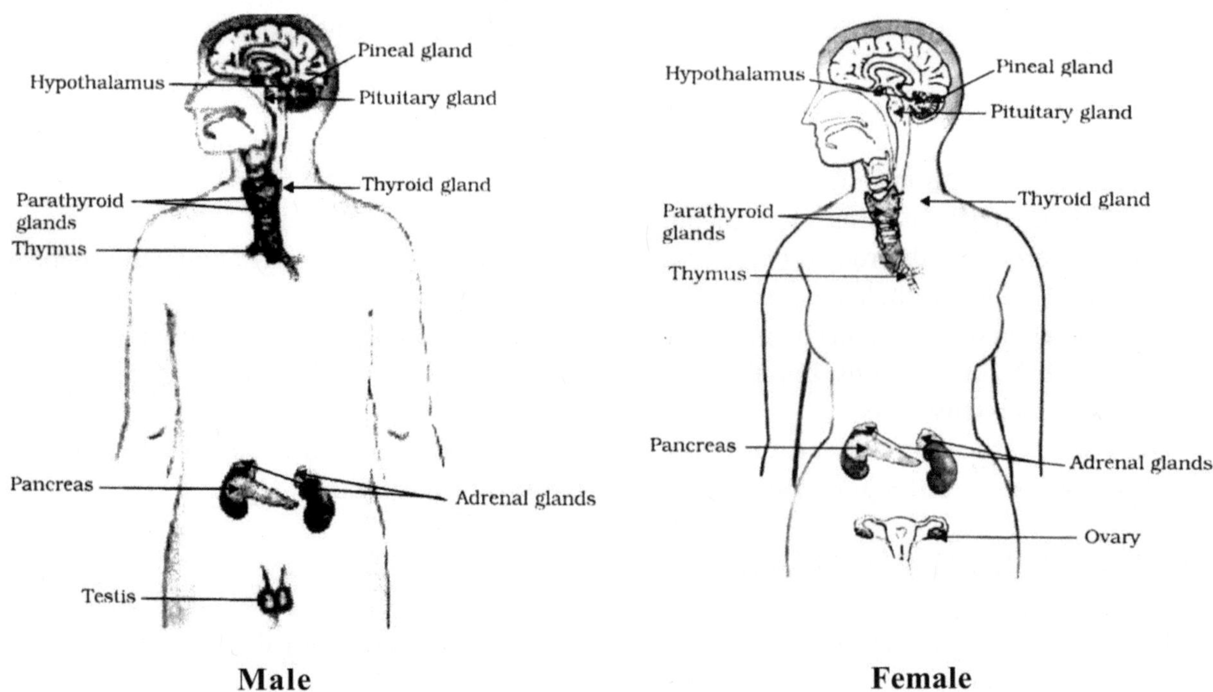

Male **Female**

- They lack ducts and pour their secretion in blood.
- Thus, are also known as ductless glands.
- The following are the major endocrine glands in human body:

- Hypothalamus, pituitary (hypophysis), pineal, thyroid, parathyroid, pancreas, adrenal, testes (in males) and ovaries (in females).
- Some endocrine glands like pancreas, testis and ovary are, both exocrine and endocrine in function. So, these are called **mixed glands** or **heterocrine glands.**

(i) Hypothalamus

- It is present in the fore brain.
- It regulates the secretion of hormones from pituitary gland and it produces releasing hormones, so it is also known as 'Master of master endocrine gland'. **Hypothalamus secretes ADH (vasopressin) and Oxytocin (Birth Hormone).**
- Vasopressin hormone regulates water and electrolyte balance in the body. Its deficiency causes **diabetes incipidus**.
- Oxytocin hormone regulates the ejection of milk during lactation. It is also known as **birth hormone** as it cause contraction of smooth muscles of uterus during child birth.

(ii) Pituitary gland (Hypophysis)

- It is present at the base of the fore brain. It is also known as the **master endocrine** gland as it controls all the other endocrine glands of the body. The pituitary gland mainly secretes following hormones.
- **Growth Hormone (GH)** regulates the growth and development of bones and muscles. Excess secretion of GH causes 'gigantism' while less secretion causes 'dwarfism'.
- **Trophic hormones** regulate the secretion of hormones from other endocrine glands like adrenal glands, thyroid gland, testes and ovaries.
- **Prolactin hormone** regulates the function of mammary glands in females.

(iii) Pineal gland

- It is known as biological clock of the body.
- It is present in the brain near to the pituitary gland.
- It secretes melatonin hormone which delays sexual development and induce sleep.

(iv) Thyroid gland

- It is present in the neck on either side of trachea. It consists of two lobes joined by isthmus. It produces **thyroxine.**
- Regulate BMR or Basal Metabollic Rate in body.
- Iodine is necessary for the thyroid gland to make thyroxin, so lack of Iodine cause swelling in thyroid gland **(Goiter).**
- Soil of hilly areas is deficit of iodine. So, hilly areas are regarded as **goiter belt**.
- Thyroxin regulates the metabolism of carbohydrates, fats and proteins in the body so as to provide the best balance for growth.
- It also regulates metamorphosis in tadpole larvae of frogs.

(v) Parathyroid glands

- These are four in number and are embedded in the thyroid gland.
- They secrete a hormone called **calcitonin** or **parathormone**.
- It regulates calcium and phosphate levels in the blood (moves calcium from bones to blood). Hence, increases calcium level in blood.

(vi) Thymus

- It is paired structure present in chest.
- It secretes the hormone **thymosin** which activates immune responses and helps in the production of antibodies.
- This gland degenerates when sexual maturity is attained.

(vii) Adrenal glands

- These are two in number, they are located one on top of each kidney. So are also called **supra-renal glands.**
- Internally these consist of two parts **outer cortex** and **inner medulla** which secretes **corticoids** and **adrenaline** hormone respectively.
- Corticoide hormones regulate carbohydrate metabolism, mineral balance and sexual development in the body.
- Adrenaline hormone is secreted in emergency or stress condition and regulate heart beat, breathing rate, blood pressure etc. in the body. It works on the principle of flight, fright and fight. So the gland is also known as **3F gland**.
- This gland is related with sex, sugar, salt, stress, so also called as **4S gland**.

(viii) Pancreas

- It is present just below the stomach in between both limbs of duodenum in the body.
- Pancreas is mixed gland (exocrine as well as endocrine gland). The endocrine parts are called **islets of langerhans.**
- It secretes two hormones-**insulin and glucagon**.
- The function of insulin hormone is to lower the blood glucose as it converts sugar into glycogen.
- The function of glucagon hormone is to increase the blood glucose as it converts glycogen into sugar.

$$\text{Sugar} \underset{\text{Glucagons}}{\overset{\text{Insulin}}{\rightleftharpoons}} \text{Glycogen}$$

(ix) Testes

- In males, testes are present outside the abdomen cavity in scrotum. These produce male hormone and male gametes.
- They secrete male sex hormone called **testosterone.**
- The function of testosterone is to regulate development of male accessory sex organs and secondary sexual characters of male like moustache, beard and voice.

(x) Ovaries

- In female, ovaries are present in the lower abdomen. These perform dual function of producing female gametes as well as female sex hormones.
- They secrete two female sex hormones called **estrogen and progesterone**.
- The function of estrogen hormone is to regulate the development of female accessory sex organs and secondary sexual characters of female such as mammary glands, soft skin, hair pattern and feminine voice.
- The function of progesterone hormone is to control the changes in uterus during menstrual cycle. It also helps in the maintenance of pregnancy.

DIFFERENT ENDOCRINE GLANDS, THEIR LOCATION IN THE BODY & THE HORMONES SECRETED BY THEM.

S.NO.	DIFFERENT ENDOCRINE GLANDS	LOCATION	HORMONES SECRETED
(A)	Pituitary	Located below Hypothalamus	→ Anterior lobe → Somatotropic hormone(SH/GH) (Growth Hormone); → Follicle stimulating hormone(FSH); → Leutinizing hormone(LH); → Adrenocorticotropic hormone(ACTH); → Thyroid stimulating hormone(TSH); → Prolactin → Middle → Melanocyte stimulating hormone (MSH) → Posterior lobe → Vasopressin/Anti Diuretic Hormone (ADH); → Oxytocin
(B)	Pineal gland	Located between cerebral hemispheres.	→ Melatonin → Serotonin
(C)	Thyroid	It surrounds the larynx & upper part of the trachea in the neck	→ Thyroxine → Calcitonin
(D)	Parathyroid	Situated on lobes of the thyroid gland.	→ Parathormone
(E)	Thymus gland	Located in the upper part of the thorax near heart.	→ Thymosin
(F)	Pancreas	Pancreas lies below the stomach in a bend of the duodenum.	→ Insulin,Glucagon and Somatostatin (Islets of Langerhans)
(G)	Adrenal gland	Located on the top of kidneys.	→ Adrenal cortex → Mineralo corticoids; → Sex hormones; → Gluco corticoids → Adrenal medulla → Adrenaline; Noradrenaline
(H)	Gonads	→ Ovaries (Female) - Located in pelvic cavity in abdomen. → Testes (Male) extra-abdominal in position	→ Estrogen; → Progesterone; → Relaxin → Testosterone

HOMEOSTASIS AND FEED BACK

- Homeostasis is the maintenance of steady state inside the organism irrespective of changes in the environment.
- Hormones maintain homeostasis by their integrated action and feed back control.
  Example: – Hormone thyroxin regulates the rate of chemical activities of the cells or regulate BMR of the body. It is produced by thyroid gland and is passed into blood.
- Thyroxin is produced under the influence of **thyroid stimulating hormone (TSH)** produced by anterior pituitary gland.
- Anterior Pituitary in turn is stimulated by **thyrotrophic releasing hormone (TRH)** produced by the hypothalamus.
- The level of thyroxin is guard by hypothalamus.
- If the level of thyroxine is higher in blood it gives **negative feed back** to the hypothalamus.
- Which stops forming TRH which stops production of TSH by pituitary.
- No thyroxine is secreated by Thyroid untill its level becomes normal.
- When level of thyroxine is lower in blood, **positive feed back** is given to hypothalamus.
- Hypothalamus starts forming more thyrotrophic releasing hormones, which stimulates the production of TSH by the pituitary.
- So, now thyroid is stimulated by TSH to produce more thyroxin in blood untill its level becomes normal in blood.

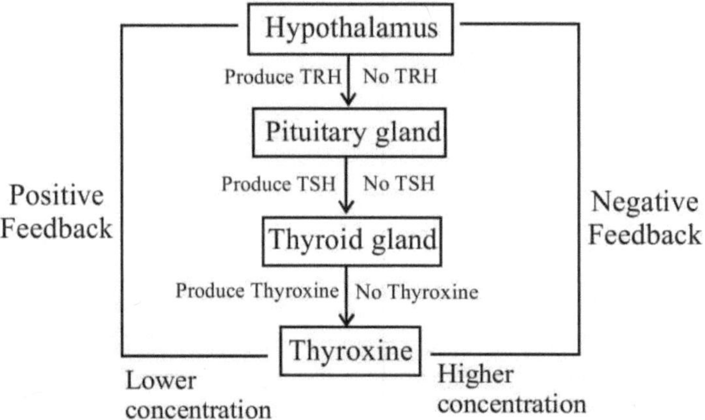

TRY YOURSELF

1. Olfactory reception is related to sense of :
   (A) Smelling (B) Tasting (C) Hearing (D) Vision

2. Axon are :
   (A) Impulse (B) Cytoplasmic extension
   (C) Part of muscles (D) All are correct

3. Receptor for stimulus are present in :
   (A) Stomach (B) Response (C) Sense organ (D) Hot objects

4. Impulse is generated when
   (A) Response is over (B) Response is going to be over
   (C) Stimulus is gained (D) Stimulus is over

5. CNS consists of :
   (A) Brain (B) Spinal Cord (C) Both (A) and (B) (D) None of these

6. Which among them is not a voluntary action of body :
   (A) Writing (B) Talking (C) Walking (D) Breathing

7. Cranium is related to :
   (A) Head (B) Thorax (C) Abdomen (D) Limbs

8. Response in plant are regulated by :
   (A) Sunlight (B) Gravity (C) Air (D) Phytohormone

9. Animals have specialized protein that helps in movement. Plant show movement due to change in :
   (A) nature of plasma membrane (B) amount of water
   (C) amount of enzyme (D) none of these

10. Movement of pollen tubes towards ovule is an example of :
    (A) Geotropism (B) Hydrotropism (C) Chemotropism (D) Phototropic

11. Unlike tropisms, nastic movements are in response to :
    (A) Darkness (B) Wind
    (C) Non-directional stimuli (D) Directional stimuli

12. Roots grow downward as a ________ response.
    (A) Positive phototropic (B) Negative phototropic
    (C) Negative geotropic (D) All of these

13. Ripening of fruits, such as bananas, is hastened by :
    (A) Gibberellins (B) Abscisic acid (C) Cytokinin (D) Ethylene

14. A human hormone reducing blood flow to the digestive system and skin during stress is :
    (A) Thyroxin (B) Adrenaline (C) Growth hormone (D) Insulin

15. Hormone associated with gonads :
(A) Testosterone (B) Estrogen (C) Auxin (D) Both (A) and (B)

16. Name the hormone which controls the basal metabolic rate in animals.
(A) Adrenaline (B) Thyroxine (C) Aldosterone (D) Oxytocin

17. ________ is responsible for maintaining biological clock of body :
(A) Pineal (B) Kidney (C) Thyroid (D) Adrenal

18. Deficiency of ______ cause dwarfism
(A) GH (B) FSH (C) LH (D) All of these

19. A person consuming sea food is least likely to develop :
(A) Diabetes (B) Goiter (C) Both A and B (D) Heart Diseases

20 A patient of diabetes is not producing :
(A) Insulin (B) Thyroxin (C) Oestrogen (D) Adrenaline

21. Growth hormone is produced by :
(A) Adrenal (B) Pituitary (C) Pancreas (D) Thyroid

POINTS TO REMEMBER

1. A system of control and coordination is essential in living organisms so that the different body parts can function as a single unit to maintain homeostasis as well as respond to various stimuli.
2. In animals, the nervous system and hormonal system are responsible for control and coordination.
3. Neurons are specialized cells of the nervous system. They use electrical and chemical signals for transferring information.
4. Receptors are specialized tips of the nerve fibres that collect the information to be conducted by the nerves.
5. Nerve impulses travel in the following manner from one neuron to the next :
   Dendrites → Cell body → Axon → Nerve endings at the tip of axon → Synapse → Dendrite of next neuron.
6. Chemicals released from axon tip of one neuron, cross the synapse or neuromuscular junction to reach the next cell (neuron or muscle fibre).
7. Nerve impulses from many neurons interact to carry out the complex process of thinking.
8. Central nervous system and peripheral nervous system are parts of our nervous system.
9. Central nervous system is made up of the brain and spinal cord. Get the Power of Visual Impact on your side
10. Spinal cord controls the reflex actions and conducts messages between different parts of the body and brain.
11. Reflex action is an automatic, rapid and immediate reaction to a stimulus and is below the level of consciousness. No thinking is involved in reflex action.
12. Reflex arc is the neural pathway that mediates a reflex action.
    Pathway of reflex arc :
    Receptor → Sensory neuron → Relay neuron → Motor neuron → Effector
13. The sensory neurons of reflex arcs synapse in the spinal cord which then activates the spinal motor neurons without delay to execute a quick action, especially in case of emergencies. The brain also receives the information while the reflex action occurs.
14. The 3 main parts of the brain are forebrain, midbrain and hindbrain.
15. The largest part of the brain, the forebrain, is the main thinking region. It is made up of cerebrum, hypothalamus and thalamus. Cerebellum, pons and medulla constitute the hindbrain.
16. Cerebrum is the largest part of the brain whereas the cerebellum is the second largest part.
17.

Part of brain	Function
Cerebrum	Governs intelligence, thinking, memory and other mental abilities, voluntary actions, sensations, emotions and speech
Hypothalamus	Coordinates messages from the autonomous nervous system, controls certain involuntary actions, as well as the sexual and emotional behaviour and forms an axis with the pituitary
Thalamus	Functions as major coordinating center for sensory and motor signaling.
Midbrain	Acts as the coordinating centre between forebrain and hindbrain; also controls certain involuntary movements
Cerebellum	Responsible for precision and fine control of voluntary movements as well as maintaining posture and equilibrium of the body
Pons	Relays impulses between the lower cerebellum and spinal cord, and higher parts of the brain like the cerebrum and mid brain; also regulates respiration
Medulla	Contains vital centres for controlling blood pressure, respiration, swallowing, salivation, vomiting, sneezing and coughing.

18. Brain is protected by a bony box called **cranium**, within which are present 3 layers of fluid-filled membranes for absorbing shock.
19. Peripheral nervous system consists of cranial nerves and spinal nerves and assists in transmitting information between central nervous system and rest of the body.
20. Reflex actions, voluntary actions and involuntary actions are the various types of responses shown by the nervous system.
21. The sense organs detect changes in surroundings and pass this information to the central nervous system, which after processing the information, acts through the muscles.
22. The movements of muscle tissues are brought about by the contraction and relaxation of the contractile proteins in response to nerve impulses.
23. Plants lack nervous and muscular system.
24. Plants respond to stimuli by showing 2 types of movements – growth independent and growth dependent.
25. Growth independent movements are usually quicker than growth dependent ones, and involve the use of electrochemical signals by the plant. To achieve this movement, the plant cells change shape by altering their water content.
26. Growth dependent movements or tropic movements are slow, occurring either towards or away from the stimulus.
27. Tropic movements are shown in response to environmental factors such as light, gravity, water and chemicals.
28. Plant roots are positively geotropic and negatively phototropic whereas plant shoots are usually negatively geotropic and positively phototropic.
29. Pollen tubes show chemotropism by growing towards the ovules.
30. In addition to electrochemical signals, plants and animals use hormones for control and coordination.
31. Important plant hormones are auxin, gibberellin, cytokinin, abscisic acid and ethylene.

Plant hormone	Function
Auxin	Cell elongation
Cytokinin	Cell division
Gibberellin	Growth of stem
Abscisic acid	Inhibits growth
Ethylene	Ripening of fruits

32. Auxin causes the bending of plant stem towards light as well as the curling of plant tendrils around a support.
33. Animal hormones do not bring about directional growth depending on environmental cues, but promote controlled growth in various areas to maintain the body design.
34. The various endocrine glands in humans are hypothalamus, pineal gland, pituitary gland, thyroid gland, parathyroid glands, thymus, pancreas, adrenal glands, ovary (in female) and testis (in males).
35. Some important hormones and their functions in human body :

Hormone	Endocrine gland	Function
Growth hormone	Pituitary	Regulates growth and development of body
Thyroxin	Thyroid gland	Controls carbohydrate, protein and fat metabolism
Adrenaline	Adrenal gland	Prepares the body to deal with emergency situations
Insulin	Pancreas	Regulates blood sugar levels
Testosterone	Testis	Causes development of sexual organs and secondary sexual characteristics in males
Oestrogen	Ovary	Causes development of sexual organs and secondary sexual characteristics in females

36. In case of flight or fight reaction to an emergency situation,
Adrenal glands → release adrenaline into blood → which acts on heart and other tissues → causes faster heart beat → more oxygen to muscles → reduced blood supply to digestive system and skin → diversion of blood to skeletal muscles → increase in breathing rate.
37. Deficiency of iodine causes goiter whereas deficiency of growth hormone and insulin causes dwarfism and diabetes respectively.
38. Feedback mechanisms are present to regulate the hormone action.
39. Difference between nervous and endocrine system.

	Nervous system	**Endocrine system**
Mode of communication	Electrical impulses	Chemical compounds
Speed of communication	Very quick	Slow
Can reach	Only cells connected by nervous system	All cells of the body
Continuity	Cannot continuously transmit impulses	Can act steadily and persistently

40. Nervous system is absent in sponges.
41. In Hydra Nerve net (primitive nervous system made up of similar neurons) is present.
42. In Planaria rudimentary brain is present.
43. Vertebrates have well developed brain and nervous system.
44. Fully form neurons loose the power of divison and thus formation of new neurons shortly after the birth.
45. Jagdish Chandra Bose first showed that plant shows movement and feels pain.
46. Brain is protected in three membranes i.e. Duramater, Piamater and Arachnoid.
47. A useful acronym to summarize the function of the autonomous nervous system is STUDD (salivation, tear, urination, digestion and defecation).
48. **Senescence :** Disappearance of chlorophyll and degradation of proteins are two impotant symptoms of senescence. Cytokinins delay these processes and thus the senescence is also delayed. This effect of cytokinins is known as Richmond-Lang Effect.

CONCEPT APPLICATION LEVEL - I [NCERT Questions]

Q.1. What is the difference between a reflex action and walking?

Ans. A reflex action is a rapid, automatic response to a stimulus. It does not involve any thinking. For example, we close our eyes immediately when the bright light is focused. Walking, on the other hand, is a voluntary action. It is under our conscious control.

Q.2 What happens at the synapse between two neurons?

Ans. A very small gap that occurs between the last portion of axon of one neuron and the dendron of the other neuron is known as a synapse. It acts as a one way valve to transmit impulses in one direction only. This uni-direction transfer of impulses occurs as the chemicals are produced in only one side of the neuron i.e., the axon's side. From axon, the impulses travel across the synapse to the dendron of the other neuron.

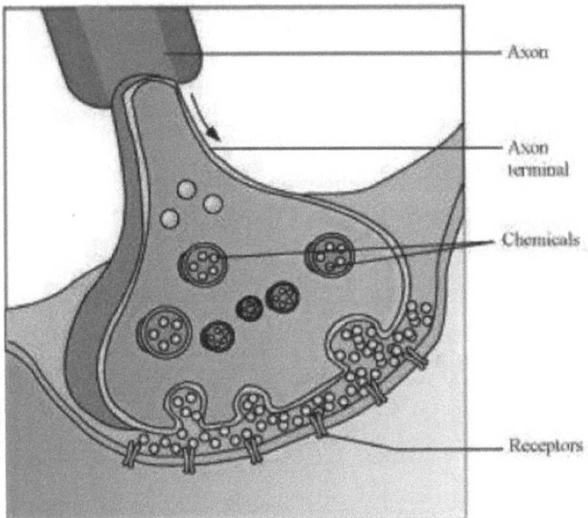

A synapse or neuromuscular junction

Q.3 Which part of the brain maintains posture and equilibrium of the body?

Ans. Cerebellum, a part of hindbrain is responsible for maintaining posture and equilibrium of the body.

Q.4 How do we detect the smell of an agarbatti (incense stick)?

Ans. The thinking part of our brain is the forebrain. It has separate areas that are specialized for hearing, smelling, sight, taste, touch, etc. The forebrain also has regions that collect information or impulses from the various receptors. When the smell of an incense stick reaches us, our forebrain detects it. Then, the forebrain interprets it by putting it together with the information received from other receptors and also with the information already stored in the brain.

Q.5. What is the role of the brain in reflex action?

Ans. Reflex actions are sudden responses, which do not involve any thinking. For example, when we touch a hot object, we withdraw our hand immediately without thinking as thinking may take time which would be enough to get us burnt. The sensory nerves that detect the heat are connected to the nerves that move the muscles of the hand. Such a connection of detecting the signal from the nerves (input) and responding to it quickly (output) is called a reflex arc. The reflex arcs -connections present between the input and output nerves - meet in a bundle in the spinal cord.

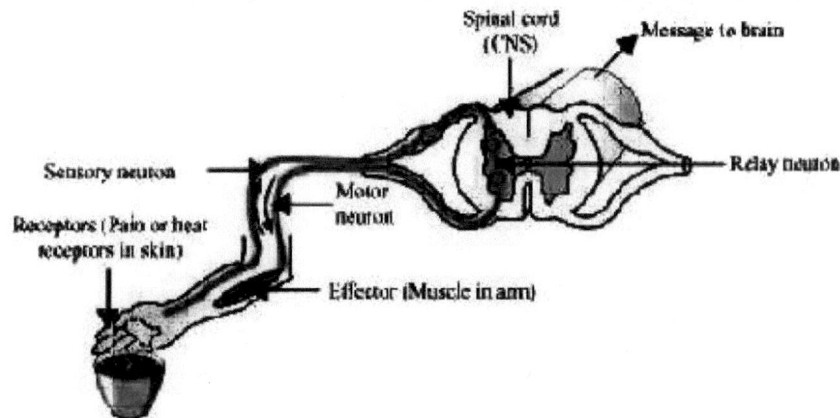

Reflex arc

Reflex arcs are formed in the spinal cord and the information (input) reaches the brain. The brain is only aware of the signal and the response that has taken place. However, the brain has no role to play in the creation of the response.

Q.6 What are plant hormones?

Ans. Plant hormones or phytohormones are naturally-occurring organic substances. These are synthesized in one part of the plant body (in minute quantities) and are translocated to other parts when required. The five major types of phytohormones are auxins, gibberellins, cytokinins, abscisic acid, and ethylene.

Q.7 How is the movement of leaves of the sensitive plant different from the movement of a shoot towards light?

Ans. The movement of leaves of the sensitive plant, Mimosa pudica or "touch me not", occurs in response to touch or contact stimuli. This movement is independent of growth. The movement of shoot towards light is known as phototropism. This type of movement is directional and is growth dependent.

Q.8 Give an example of a plant hormone that promotes growth.

Ans. Auxin is an example of growth-promoting plant hormone.

Q.9 How do auxins promote the growth of a tendril around a support?

Ans. Auxin is synthesized at the shoot tip. It helps the cell grow longer. When a tendril comes in contact with a support, auxin stimulates faster growth of the cells on the opposite side, so that the tendril forms a coil around the support. This makes the tendrils appear as a watch spring.

Q.10 Design an experiment to demonstrate hydrotropism.

Ans. Take two small beakers and label them as A and B. Fill beaker A with water. Now make a cylindrical-shaped roll from a filter paper and keep it as a bridge between beaker A and beaker B, as shown in the figure. Attach few germinating seeds in the middle of the filter. Now, cover the entire set-up with a transparent plastic container so that the moisture is retained.

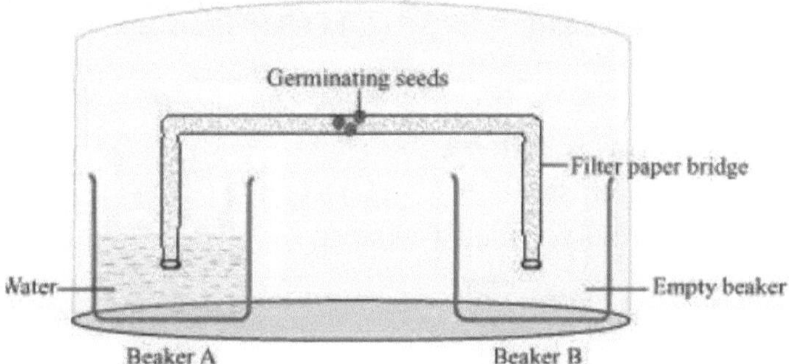

Observation:

The roots of the germinating seeds will grow towards beaker A.

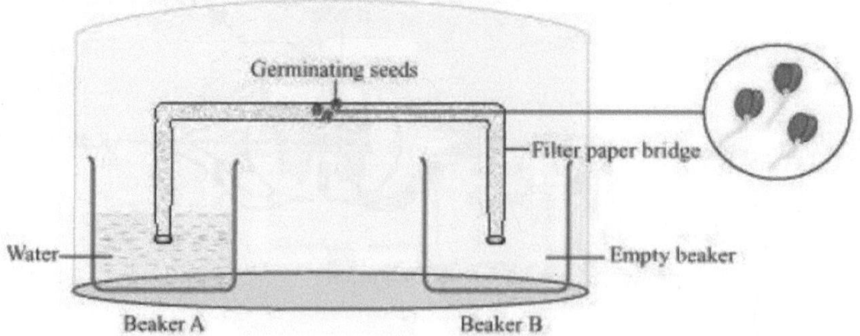

This experiment demonstrates the phenomenon of hydrotropism.

Q.11 How does chemical coordination take place in animals?

Ans. Chemical coordination takes place in animals with the help of hormones.Hormone is the chemical messenger that regulates the physiological processes in living organisms. It is secreted by glands. The regulation of physiological processes, and control and coordination by hormones comes under the endocrine system. The nervous system along with the endocrine system in our body controls and coordinates the physiological processes.

Q.12 Why is the use of iodised salt advisable?

Ans. Iodine stimulates the thyroid gland to produce thyroxin hormone. It regulates carbohydrate, fat, and protein metabolism in our body. Deficiency of this hormone results in the enlargement of the thyroid gland. This can lead to goitre, a disease characterized by swollen neck. Therefore, iodised salt is advised for normal functioning of the thyroid gland.

Q.13 How does our body respond when adrenaline is secreted into the blood?

Ans. Adrenalin is a hormone secreted by the adrenal glands in case of any danger or emergency or any kinds of stress. It is secreted directly into the blood and is transported to different parts of the body. When secreted in large amounts, it speeds up the heartbeat and hence supplies more oxygen to the muscles. The breathing rate also increases due to contractions of diaphragm and rib muscles. It also increases the blood pressure. All these responses enable the body to deal with any stress or emergency.

Q.14 Why are some patients of diabetes treated by giving injections of insulin?

Ans. Diabetes is a disease in which the level of sugar in the blood is too high. Insulin, a hormone secreted by the pancreas, helps in regulating the blood sugar levels. This is the reason why diabetic patients are treated by giving injections of insulin.

Q.15 Which of the following is a plant hormone?

(A) Insulin **(B) Thyroxin** **(C) Oestrogen** **(D) Cytokinin**

Ans. (D) Cytokinin is a plant hormone.

Q.16 The gap between two neurons is called a

(A) dendrite. **(B) synapse.** **(C) axon.** **(D) impulse.**

Ans. (B) The gap between two neurons is called a synapse.

Q.17 The brain is responsible for

(A) thinking **(B) regulating the heart beat**

(C) balancing the body. **(D) all of the above.**

Ans. (D) The brain is responsible for thinking, regulating the heart beat and balancing the body.

Q.18 What is the function of receptors in our body? Think of situations where receptors do not work properly. What problems are likely to arise?

Ans. Receptors are sensory structures (organs/tissues or cells) present all over the body. The receptors are either grouped in case of eye or ear, or scattered in case of skin. Functions of receptors:
(i) They sense the external stimuli such as heat or pain.
(ii) They also trigger an impulse in the sensory neuron which sends message to the spinal cord.
When the receptors are damaged, the external stimuli transferring signals to the brain are not felt. For example, in the case of damaged receptors, if we accidentally touch any hot object, then our hands might get burnt as damaged receptors cannot perceive the external stimuli of heat and pain.

Q.19 Draw the structure of a neuron and explain its function.

Ans. Neurons are the functional units of the nervous system. The three main parts of a neuron are axon, dendrite, and cell body.

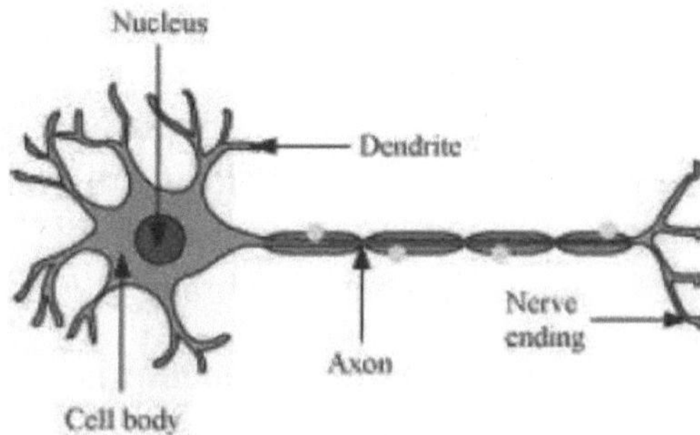

Structure of a neuron

Functions of the three parts of a neuron:
Axon: It conducts messages away from the cell body.
Dendrite: It receives information from axon of another cell and conducts the messages towards the cell body.
Cell body : It contains nucleus, mitochondria, and other organelles. It is mainly concerned with the maintenance and growth.

Q.20 What are the changes seen in girls at the time of puberty?

Ans. Secondary sexual characteristics in girls:
- Increase in breast size and darkening of skin of the nipples present at the tips of the breasts.
- Appearance of hair in the genital area.
- Appearance of hair in other areas of skin like underarms, face, hands, and legs.
- Increase in the size of uterus and ovary.
- Beginning of menstrual cycle.
- More secretion of oil from the skin, which results in the appearance of pimples.

Q.21 Which signals will get disrupted in case of a spinal cord injury?

Ans. The reflex arc connections between the input and output nerves meet in a bundle in the spinal cord. In fact, nerves from all over the body meet in a bundle in the spinal cord on their way to the brain. In case of any injury to the spinal cord, the signals coming from the nerves as well as the signals coming to the receptors will be disrupted.

Q.22 How does chemical coordination occur in plants?

Ans. In animals, control and coordination occur with the help of nervous system. However, plants do not have a nervous system. Plants respond to stimuli by showing movements. The growth, development, and responses to the environment in plants is controlled and coordinated by a special class of chemical substances known as hormones. These hormones are produced in one part of the plant body and are translocated to other needy parts. For example, a hormone produced in roots is translocated to other parts when required. The five major types of phytohormone are auxins, gibberellins, cytokinins, abscisic acid, and ethylene. These phytohormones are either growth promoters (such as auxins, gibberellins, cytokinins, and ethylene) or growth inhibitors such as abscisic acid.

Q.23 What is the need for a system of control and coordination in an organism?

Ans. The maintenance of the body functions in response to changes in the body by working together of various integrated body systems is known as coordination. All the movements that occur in response to stimuli are carefully coordinated and controlled. In animals, the control and coordination movements are provided by nervous and muscular systems. The nervous system sends messages to and away from the brain. The spinal cord plays an important role in the relay of messages. In the absence of this system of control and coordination, our body will not be able to function properly. For example, when we accidentally touch a hot utensil, we immediately withdraw our hand. In the absence of nerve transmission, we will not withdraw our hand and may get burnt.

Q.24 How are involuntary actions and reflex actions different from each other?

Ans. Involuntary actions cannot be consciously controlled. For example, we cannot consciously control the movement of food in the alimentary canal. These actions are however directly under the control of the brain. On the other hand, the reflex actions such as closing of eyes immediately when bright light is focused show sudden response and do not involve any thinking. This means that unlike involuntary actions, the reflex actions are not under the control of brain.

Q.25 Compare and contrast nervous and hormonal mechanisms for control and coordination in animals.

Ans. Nervous system mechanism Hormonal system mechanism

Nervous system mechanism	Hormonal system mechanism
The information is conveyed in the form of electric impulse.	The information is conveyed in the form of chemical messengers.
The axons and dendrites transmit the information through a coordinated effort.	The information is transmitted or transported through blood.
The flow of information is rapid and the response is quick.	The information travels slowly and the response is slow.
Its effects are short lived.	It has prolonged effects.

Q.26 What is the difference between the manner in which movement takes place in a sensitive plant and the movement in our legs?

Ans.

Movement in sensitive plants	Movement in our legs
The movementthat takes place in a sensitive plant such as *Mimosa pudica* occurs in response to touch (stimulus).	Movement in our legs is an example of voluntary actions.
For this movement, the information is transmitted from cell to cell by electrochemical signals as plants do not have any specialised tissue for conduction of impulses.	The signal or messages for these actions are passed to the brain and hence are consciously controlled.
For this movement to occur, the plant cells change shape by changing the amount of water in them.	In animal muscle cells, some proteins are found which allow the movement to occur.

CONCEPT APPLICATION LEVEL - II

SECTION-A

- **Fill in the blanks**

1. The central nervous system consists of the ___________ and ___________.
2. ___________reduce blood sugar
3. ___________gland is embedded in thyroid gland.
4. ___________ is synthesised at shoot tip.
5. ___________inhibit growth in plant.
6. Brain is present in ___________which is part of skull.
7. ___________functions are controlled by medulla.

SECTION – B

1. The bending of shoot tip towards light is known as
(A) Geotropism (B) Phototropism (C) Chemotropism (D) Hydrotropism

2. Which of the following gland is unpaired?
(A) Adrenal (B) Testis (C) Pituitary (D) Ovary

3. Which of the following is commonly known as 'birth hormone'?
(A) Prolactin (B) Oxytocin (C) ADH (D) FSH

4. Deficiency of Insulin causes
(A) Diabetes mellitus (B) Diabetes insipidus (C) Cretinism (D) Dwarfism

5. The structural and functional unit of nervous system is
(A) Nephron (B) Neuron (C) Cyton (D) Axon

6. Name the layers of brain from inside towards the outside
(A) Duramater, Arachnoid and Piamater (B) Arachnoid, Duramater and Piamater
(C) Piamater, Arachnoid and Duramater (D) Arachnoid, Piamater and Duramater

7. One of the following is not a reflex action
(A) Knee Jerk (B) Boxing (C) Coughing (D) Eye lid closing

8. Which among them is a reflex arc
(A) Sensory neuron → Motor neuron → Relay neuron
(B) Motor neuron → relay → motor neuron
(C) Sensory → relay → motor neuron
(D) Relay → Motor → Sensory

9. Hypothalamus is a part of
(A) Fore brain (B) Mid brain (C) Hind brain (D) Medulla

10. While writing on a wall, what type of muscle are used
(A) Cardice (B) Voluntary (C) Involuntary (D) Brain

11. Drooping of leaf in Mimosa plant is
(A) due to dependence on growth (B) movement independent of growth
(C) due to loss of turgidity (D) Both (B) & (C)

12. While touching a hot plate, a reflex action is seen what is the effector in it
(A) Skin (B) Spinal cord (C) Muscle (D) Brain

13. Iodine is necessary for the synthesis of which hormone ?
(A) Adrenaline (B) Thyroxin (C) Auxin (D) Insulin

14. Choose the incorrect statement about insulin :
(A) It is produced from pancreas (B) It regulates growth and development of the body
(C) It regulates blood sugar level (D) Insufficient secretion of insulin will cause diabetes.

15. Select the mis-matched pair :
(A) Adrenaline : Pituitary gland (B) Testosterone : Testes
(C) Estrongen : Ovary (D) Thyroxine : Thyroid gland

16. The shape of guard cells changes due to change in the :
(A) protein composition of cells (B) Temperature of cells
(C) Amount of water in cells (D) Position of nucleus in the cells

17. The growth of tendril in pea plants is due to :
(A) Effect of light
(B) Effect of gavity
(C) Rapid cell divisions in tendrillar cells that are away from the support.
(D) Rapid cell divisions in tendrillar cells in contact with the support.

18. The movement of sunflower in accordance with the path of sun is due to :
(A) Phototropism (B) Geotropism (C) Chemotropism (D) Hydrotropism.

19. The substance that triggers the fall of mature leaves and fruits from plant is due to :
(A) Auxin (B) Gibberellin (C) Abscisis acid (D) Cytokinin.

SECTION – C
CHECK YOUR COMPATIBILITY

[Very Very Short answer question 1 Marks Each]

1. Name the two mechanisms which control and coordinate the activites of the different parts of the body.
2. Name the master gland of the body.
3. Name the hormone which stimulates growth of milk glands and milk secretion.
4. Name the largest endocrine gland.
5. Name the hormones produced by Pancreas.
6. Name the disease, which is caused due to deficiency of insulin.
7. Write the full form of : (a) PNS (b) CNS (c) TSH (d) TRH
8. Mention the three layers of meninges from outside to inside.
9. Name the part of brain which controls equilibrium and posture of body.
10. Name the part of hind brain which takes part in regulation of respiration.

11. We suddenly withdraw our hand when a pin pricks. Name the type of response involved in this action.
12. Which hormone is responsible for the development of moustache and beard in men?
13. Give four functions of plant hormones.

[Very Short answer question (2 Marks)]

14. Why is abscisic acid known as stress hormone?
15. Distinguish between nastic and tropic movement.
16. Explain the feedback control mechanism of hormones.
17. Name the box in which brain is situated. What is the weight of fully grown human brain?
18. Name the largest and second largest part of the brain.
19. If one fruit is ripened and if it is kept in a basket of raw fruits, then what will happen? What is the cause of it.
20. Name the four lobes of cerebrum and gives its functions.
21. What are phytohormones? Name any two phytohormones.

[Short answer question 3 Marks]

22. What is the endocrine control in the 'fight and flight' response? Explain.
23. Nervous and hormonal system together perform the function of control and coordination in human beings. Justify the statement.
24. Define 'nerve impluse'. Which structure in a neuron helps to conduct a nerve impulse.
    (i) towards the cell body? (ii) away from the cell body?

[Long answer question 5 Marks Each]

25. Name the different endocrine glands in the human body. Mention the roles they play in the human body, giving names of the hormones secreted.
26. Explain the structure of a brain with the help of a suitable diagram. Give one function each of various parts of brain.

SECTION – D
PREVIOUS YEAR'S QUESTIONS

Very Short Answer Type Questions : (One Mark)

Q.1 Mention the part of the brain which controls the involuntary actions like blood pressure, salivation etc.
Ans. Medulla in the hind-brain. **[SAI-2015]**

Q.2 Name the largest part of hind-brain. **[SAI-2015]**
Ans. Cerebellum.

Q.3 State the main function of abscisic acid in plants. **[SAI-2011, 2014]**
Ans. (i) It inhibits growth / germination of seeds.
(ii) It causes wilting of leaves.

Q.4 Give two functions of a neuron. **[SAI-2011, 2014]**
Ans. (i) To carry information from receptors to brain and spinal cord.
(ii) To transfer response from brain and spinal cord to effectors.

Q.5 What is synapse? **[SAI-2013, 2014]**
Ans. Synapse is the functional junction between two neurons.

Short Answer Type Questions : (Two Marks)

Q.6 A boy was not able to gain height. The doctor diagnosed that it is due to deficiency of a hormone. Name the hormone and the gland which secretes this hormone. Which disease is he suffering from? **[SAI-2015]**

Ans. • Growth hormone.
• Pituitary gland.
• Dwarfism (stunted growth).

Q.7 Give the role played by cerebellum and medulla oblongata in human brain. **[SAI-2015]**

(i) Cerebellum : It maintains the posture, muscle tone and equilibrium.

(ii) Medulla :

• It controls the rate of heart beat, breathing movements, regulation of blood pressure etc.
• It is the control centre of swallowing, coughing, sneezing and vomiting.

Q.8 State the role of the brain in reflex action. **[SAI-2013, 2014]**

Ans. The sensory area of brain receives information, interprets it and makes a rapid decision. The message is transmitted to the motor area. The motor neuron sends information to the receptor organ. The entire process is controlled by medulla oblongata in the hind-brain.

Q.9 Name the hormone secreted by human testes. State its functions. **[SAI-2012, 2014]**

Ans. (i) Testosterone.

(ii) **Functions :**

(a) It is responsible for the formation of sperms.

(b) It causes changes in the appearance of body at the time of puberty.

Short Answer Type Questions : (Three Marks)

Q.10 (a) Name the bony structure in which the following organs are protected:

(i) Brain (ii) Spinal cord

(b) Mention the main thinking part of the brain and write its three functions. **[SAI-2015]**

(a) (i) Skull (cranium)

(ii) Vertebral column

(b) • Fore-brain is the main thinking part of the brain.
• It has different areas which are specialised for hearing, smell, sight and touch etc.
• There are separate areas of association where this sensory in formation is interpreted.
• It is the main decision making area where the information is responded.

Q.11 Expand the following:

(a) ABA (b) ADH (c) TSH (d) GH (e) CNS (f) PNS

[SAI-2014]

Ans. (a) Abscisic Add

(b) Anti Diuretic Hormone

(c) Thyroid Stimulating Hormone

(d) Growth Hormone

(e) Central Nervous System

(f) Peripheral Nervous System

Long Answer Type Questions : (Five Marks)

Q.12 (a) Define reflex arc. Draw a flow chart showing the sequence of events which occur during sneezing.
(b) List four plant hormones. Write one function of each. **[SAI-2014, 2015]**

Ans. (a) The process of detecting the signal or the input and responding to it by an output action might be completed quickly. This is achieved by reflex arc.

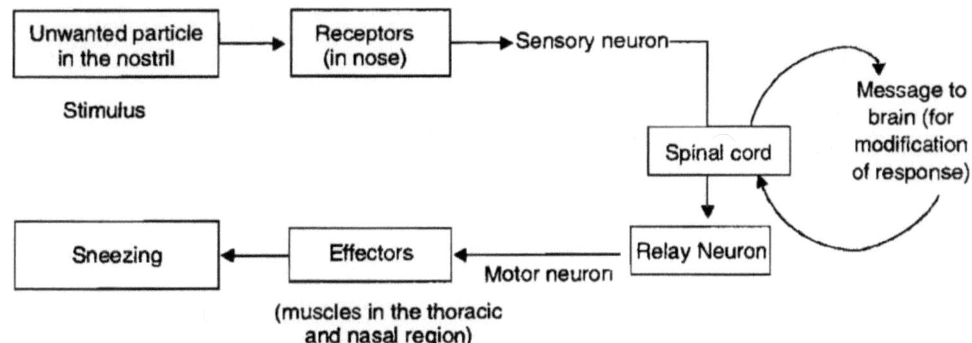

(b) Auxins -Growth hormone
Cytokinin -Promote cell division
Ethylene -Ripening of fruits.
Gibberellins -Growth of stem
Abscisic acid -Inhibits growth

Q.13 Design an experiment to demonstrate hydrotropism. **[SAI-2013, 2014, 2015]**

Ans. **Hydrotropism:** It is a response towards water. Hydrotropism is generally shown by roots only. Roots respond to differences in soil moisture content by growing toward regions of greater water potential. This tropism is called hydrotropism.

Procedure : Place germinating seeds in moist sawdust contained in a sieve.

Observations :

(i) The radicles pass down and come out of the sieve pores under the influence of gravity.
(ii) After some growth, radicles bend back and enter the sawdust again.

Conclusion drawn :

(i) This shows that roots show both hydrotropic response and geotropic response.
(ii) The hydrotropic response of root are stronger than geotropic responses.

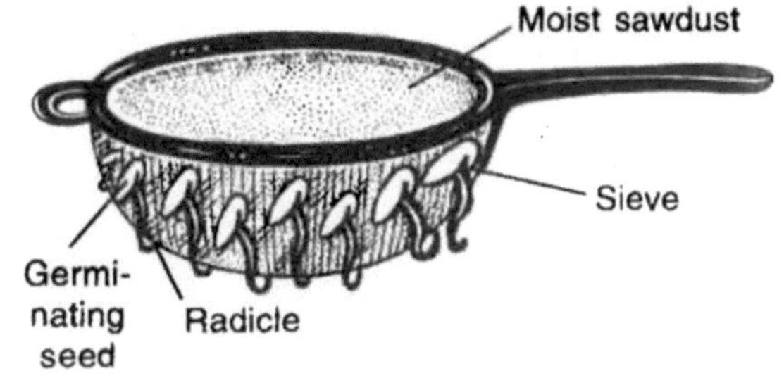

Experiment to demonstrate hydrotropism

SECTION – E
UNDERSTANDING BASED QUESTIONS

Q.1 How do the shoot and roots of a plant respond to the pull of earth's gravity ? **[SAI-2012, 2015]**

Ans. Roots grow downward towards gravity while shoot usually grows upwards and away from earth.

Q.2 State the role of the brajn in reflex action. **[SAI-2015]**

Ans. The sensory area of brain receives information, interprets it and makes a rapid decision. The message is transmitted to the motor area. The motor neuron sends information to the receptor organ (via spinal cord). This may result in the modification of response, e.g. if sneezing (a kind of reflex action) is due to the cold wind coming from a window, then brain will modify the response by closing the window which is the cause of sneezing. The entire process is controlled by medulla in the hind-brain.

Q.3 Give the functions of various parts of a neuron. **[SAI-2015]**

Ans. A neuron mainly consists of a cell body, dendrites and an elongated axon.

Functions of cyton (cell body) :

It receives stimuli from other neuron(s) through dendrites, processes the information and pass it to the axon.

Functions of dendrites: Dendrites receive electric impulses from other neurons and transfer them to the axon.

Functions of axon : Impulses travel through the axon and at the end of axon, the electrical impulses set off the release of some chemicals. So, that these impulses can be transferred to other neurons.

Q.4 Name the hormone secreted by thyroid gland. List its function. Why is the use of iodisedsalt advisable? **[SAI-2014]**

Ans. Iodine is essential for the synthesis of thyroxine hormone secreted by thyroid gland. Thyroxine regulates carbohydrate, protein and fat metabolism in the body so as to provide the best balance for growth. Deficiency of thyroxine disturbs metabolic and physical activities besides causing disorders like simple goitre. To avoid any disruption in the synthesis of thyroxine and maintaining the regular functioning of the body, consumption of iodised salt is very essential.

CONCEPT APPLICATION LEVEL - III

SECTION-A

Multiple choice question with one correct answers

1. Statoreceptors are concened with
(A) Hearing (B) Equilibrium (C) Smell (D) Taste

2. Taste receptors are
(A) Tangoreceptors (B) Gustatoreceptors (C) Olfactoreceptors (D) Photoreceptors

3. Thinking part of brain is
(A) Diencephalon (B) Hind brain (C) Mid brain (D) Fore brain

4. Most highly developed part of human brain is
(A) Cerebellum (B) Medulla (C) Cerebrum (D) Pons.

5. Spinal cord is part of
(A) Autonomic nervous system (B) Voluntary peripheral nervous system
(C) Involuntary peripheral system (D) Central nervous system.

6. Cerebellum is part of
(A) Mid brain (B) Fore brain (C) Hind brain (D) Peripheral nervous systen

7. Relay of most sensory impulses occur through
(A) Epithalamus (B) Hypothalamus (C) Thalami (D) Third ventricle

8. Number of cranial nerves is
(A) 36 (B) 24 (C) 18 (D) 12

9. In humans, number of spinal nerves is
(A) 31 pairs (B) 32 pairs (C) 33 pairs (D) 36 pairs

10. Outermost covering of brain and spinal cord is
(A) Arachnoid (B) Piamater (C) Choroid (D) Duramater

11. Part of brain that controls respiration, heart beat and peristalsis is
(A) Frontal lobe (B) Medulla oblongata (C) Occipital lobe (D) Cerebellum

12. Centre for regulating body temperature is
(A) Cerebellum (B) Medulla oblongata (C) Occipital lobe (D) Cerebellum

13. Sympathetic nervous system is component of
(A) Central nervous system (B) Voluntary peripheral
(C) Involuntary peripheral nervous system (D) Both B and C.

14. Phototropism is caused by differential distribution of
(A) IAA (B) Kinetin (C) Gibberellin (D) Abscisic acid.

15. Artificial ripening of fruits is carried out by
(A) Auxin (B) Kinetin (C) Ethylene (D) ABA

16. Nastic movements are
(A) Nondirectional (B) Directional (C) Locomotion (D) Organelle movements

17. Deficiency of insulin causes
(A) Goitre (B) Diabetes (C) Cretinism (D) Dwarfism

18. Olfactoreceptors occur in
(A) Nasal cavity (B) Buccal cavity (C) Lungs (D) Skin

19. Phonoreceptors are present is
(A) Eyes (B) Mouth (C) Ears (D) Brain

20. Centre of hearing occurs in
(A) Occipital lobes (B) Temporal lobes (C) Frontal lobes (D) Parietal lobes

SECTION-B

Assertion & Reason

Instructions: In the following questions as Assertion (A) is given followed by a Reason (R). Mark your responses from the following options.
(A) Both Assertion and Reason are true and Reason is the correct explanation of 'Assertion'
(B) Both Assertion and Reason are true and Reason is not the correct explanation of 'Assertion'
(C) Assertion is true but Reason is false
(D) Assertion is false but Reason is true

1. **Assertion:** A person has lost most of its intelligence, memory and judgement.
Reason: He undergoes operation of a tumour located in the cerebrum.

2. **Assertion:** Transmission of the nerve impulse across a synapse is accomplished by neurotransmitter.
Reason: Transmission across a synapse usually requires neurotransmitter because there is small space i.e. synaptic cleft that separates one neuron from another.

SECTION-C

Match the following (one to one)

Column-I and **column-II** contains **four** entries each. Entries of column-I are to be matched with some entries of column-II. Only One entries of column-I may have the matching with the same entries of column-II and one entry of column-II Only one matching with entries of column-I

1.

Column I	Column II
(A) Plant growth inhibitor	(P) Effector organs
(B) Motor nerve	(Q) Spinal cord
(C) Reflex action	(R) Abscisic acid
(D) Plant Growth promotor Hormone	(S) Cytokinin

SECTION-D

Comprehension

Plant hormones are broadly classified as growth promoting and growth inhibiting. Auxin responsible for apical dominance, Gibbrellin responsible for increasing internodal distance and cytokinin for cell division are growth promoting while ethylene for fruit ripening and ABA is growth inhibiting.

1. Name a gaseous hormone.
2. When shurbs tips are cut they starts spreading. Name hormone which is removed in this case?
3. Which hormone is produced during stress condition?

SECTION-E

Match the following (one to many)

Column-I and **column-II** contains **four** entries each. Entries of column-I are to be matched with some entries of column-II. One or more than one entries of column-I may have the matching with the some entries of column-II and one entry of column-II may have one or more than one matching with entries of column-I

1.

Column I	Column II
(A) Thyroxin	(P) Plant hormone
(B) Auxin	(Q) Animal hormone
(C) Oxytocin	(R) Deficiency causes Goitre
(D) Cytokinin	(S) Cell division

ANSWER KEY

Try Your Self

1.	(A)	2.	(B)	3.	(C)	4.	(C)	5.	(C)	6.	(D)	7.	(A)
8.	(D)	9.	(B)	10.	(C)	11.	(C)	12.	(B)	13.	(D)	14.	(B)
15.	(D)	16.	(B)	17.	(A)	18.	(A)	19.	(B)	20	(A)	21.	(B)

CONCEPT APPLICATION LEVEL - II

SECTION-A

1.	Brain, spinal cord	2.	Insulin	3.	Parathyroid	4.	Auxin
5.	Abscisic acid	6.	Cranium	7.	Involuntary		

SECTION - B

1.	B	2.	C	3.	B	4.	A	5.	B	6.	C	7.	B
8.	C	9.	A	10.	B	11.	D	12.	C	13.	B	14.	B
15.	A	16.	C	17.	C	18.	A	19.	C				

CONCEPT APPLICATION LEVEL - III

SECTION-A

1.	B	2.	B	3.	D	4.	C	5.	D	6.	C	7.	C
8.	B	9.	A	10.	D	11.	B	12.	C	13.	C	14.	A
15.	C	16.	A	17.	B	18.	A	19.	C	20.	B		

SECTION-B

1. A 2. A

SECTION-C

1. (A)-(R), (B)-(P), (C)-(Q), (D)-(S)

SECTION-E

1. (A)-(Q,R), (B)-(P), (C)-(Q), (D)-(P,S)

Printed by Libri Plureos GmbH in Hamburg,
Germany